MANHATTAN ARCHITECTURE

Photographs by Richard Berenholtz

———————————

Introduction by Ellen Posner

———————————

Text by Donald Martin Reynolds

———————————

PRENTICE HALL PRESS

———————————

New York   London   Toronto   Sydney   Tokyo

Prentice Hall Press
Gulf + Western Building
One Gulf + Western Plaza
New York, New York   10023

Published by the Prentice Hall Trade
Division

PRENTICE HALL PRESS and
colophon are registered trademarks
of Simon & Schuster Inc.

**Library of Congress Cataloging
in Publication Data**

Berenholtz, Richard, 1949–
    Manhattan architecture.

    Includes index.
    1. Architecture—New York
(N.Y.)   2. New York (N.Y.)—
Buildings, structures, etc.
3. Manhattan (New York, N.Y.)—
Buildings, structures, etc.
I. Reynolds, Donald M.   II. Title.
NA735.N5B47   1988
720′.9747′1   88-9850
ISBN 0-13-551987-X

Printed in Japan

10 9 8 7 6 5 4 3 2 1

First Edition

PAGE 48:

**Left, 70 Pine Street, originally the
Cities Service Building, Clinton and
Russell, 1932, and right, 40 Wall Street,
a 66-story tower whose supremacy
was eclipsed by the secret assembly of
the Chrysler Building's spire, H. Craig
Severance and Yasuo Matsui, 1929.**

RIGHT:

**A scene from St. Stephen's martyr-
dom is carved onto the north portal of
the Cathedral Church of St. John the
Divine, at Amsterdam Avenue and
112th Street.**

For my parents

1   Floral and ribbon ornament at
52 Riverside Drive.

6–7   The Great Hall of the central
wing of the Metropolitan Museum of
Art, Fifth Avenue from 80th to 83rd
streets, designed by Richard Morris
Hunt in 1902, and renovated by Roche,
Dinkeloo and Associates in 1970.

2–3   The "Chippendale" bonnet top of
the AT&T World Headquarters at 550
Madison Avenue, Philip Johnson and
John Burgee, architects, 1984.

8–9   Grant's Tomb interior, where four
coffered ceiling vaults support an
illuminated dome.

4–5   Grant's Tomb, at Riverside
Drive and West 122nd Street, John H.
Duncan, architect, 1897.

10–11   The vaulted entrance to the
International Telephone and Telegraph
Building at 67 Broad Street, by Louis
S. Weeks, 1930, has a mosaic ceiling.

12–13   The Cooper-Hewitt Museum at 2 East 91st Street was originally the Andrew Carnegie mansion. By Babb, Cook and Willard, 1903, and renovated into a museum by Hardy Holzman Pfeiffer Associates in 1977.

18–19   The World Trade Center is bounded by Church, Vesey, West, and Liberty streets. Minoru Yamasaki and Associates; Emery Roth and Sons, architects, 1970–1977.

14–15   The decorative lobby ceiling of the Trinity Building with its gilded cornice figures, 111 Broadway, by Francis H. Kimball, 1905.

20–21   The ornate detailing in the air-shaft of the Alwyn Court apartment house, 180 West 58th Street, is actually a trompe l'oeil mural of Harde and Short's original 1909 decoration, painted by Richard Haas.

16–17   The majestic interior of the Cathedral Church of St. John the Divine at Amsterdam Avenue and 112th Street, by Heins and La Farge (1892–1911), and Cram and Ferguson (1911–1942).

22–23   Bowery Savings Bank, 130 Bowery, McKim, Mead and White, 1894.

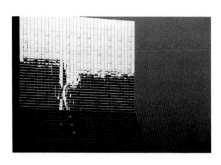

24–25   The United Nations Plaza Hotel on First Avenue and 44th Street, designed by Roche, Dinkeloo and Associates, 1976.

30–31   The iron gate at the entrance to the Apthorp, a courtyard apartment building that stretches across one block from 390 West End Avenue to 2207 Broadway, by Clinton and Russell, architects, 1908.

26–27   Wooden doors on East 95th Street.

32–33   Chanin Building: The bronze friezes by René Chambellan depict the process of life's evolution from sea to land (122 East 42nd Street, Sloan and Robertson, architects, 1929).

28–29   The iron gate at the entrance of the Morgan Library, 33 East 36th Street, by McKim, Mead and White, 1907.

34–35   The magnificent Metropolitan Life Insurance Company clock sits 350 feet up the tower at 1 Madison Avenue. It was built in 1909 by Napoleon Le Brun and completed by his sons Pierre and Michel after his death that year.

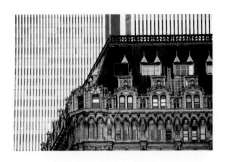

36–37   One of the financial district's essential contrasts: 90 West Street, foreground, and the World Trade Center.

42–43   Three recent midtown buildings: Citicorp Center at 153 East 53rd Street, by Hugh Stubbins and Associates, 1977; Manhattan Towers at 101 East 52nd Street, by Emery Roth and Sons, 1986; and 599 Lexington Avenue, by Edward Larrabee Barnes and Associates, 1986.

38–39   Looking skywards on Third Avenue between 53rd and 54th streets.

44–45   The fanciful City Center Fifty-Fifth Street Theater, at 131 West 55th Street, by H. P. Knowles, architect, 1924. Originally the Mecca Temple, it was built with polychromal Spanish tiles, domes, and multiple tiers.

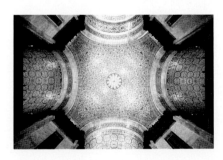

40–41   A 3-story-high ceiling of glass mosaic illuminates the lobby of the Woolworth Building at 233 Broadway, by Cass Gilbert, 1913.

46–47   Angels and Art Nouveau ornaments grace the Bayard-Condict Building at 65 Bleecker Street, by Louis Sullivan, 1898.

CONTENTS

INTRODUCTION

No single place is more emblematic of the twentieth century than Manhattan. As the flashiest component of the greater city of New York, it has come to symbolize the whole; as one of the century's great urban centers, by taking the metropolitan phenomenon to the nth degree, it has come to symbolize them all. The twentieth century's preeminent architectural symbol, the skyscraper, may not have been invented here. But on this narrow island it reached exuberant stylistic—and literal—heights.

In the early decades of this century, such structures as the Metropolitan Life tower and the Woolworth, Chrysler, and Empire State buildings captured, in dramatic and exceptionally visible ways, the corporate, commercial, and civic aspirations of their time. Their fabulous and eccentric designs, which combined romance, greed, and technology, made them international icons. Each one also reigned, in its day, as the tallest building not merely in Manhattan but on Earth.

These office buildings, as well as the proud, ornate hotel and apartment towers, the dramatic high-ceilinged banks, and the dressed-up shops and restaurants of early-twentieth-century Manhattan were not built for particularly exalted purposes but rather for the most mundane of commercial activities; that is, to facilitate the exchange of goods and services.

Still, they were built on extremely valuable real estate, in the heatedly competitive environment of a city that was approaching a dominant international role—and, as such, they were treated to every sort of architectural extravagance.

In recent years, taller, more aggressive buildings—some making larger, more abstract and quirkier gestures on the skyline and nearly all of which are made of much thinner stuff, inside and out—have made these early buildings seem almost poignantly delicate. The conglomerate of strong shapes and exotic tops, however, especially when seen at night in a delicate white beaded-and-striped web of illumination, continues to represent a triumph of artifice.

In daylight, the effect is harsher and the chaos more apparent. Cycles of demolition and new construction—in a city where change and progress have nearly always been considered the highest goods—have resulted in the loss of any number of beautiful and important buildings. And the holes have generally been filled in any-which-way so that weird, even violent, juxtapositions abound: cathedral next to sleek office tower; residential next to industrial building; carefully designed and ornamented structure next to blank speculative dud.

But daylight also reveals Manhattan's colors—its pinks, blues, greens, and silvers—and its myriad textures and materials. The Empire State Building's true character is made evident, for example, by the slim vertical strips of nickel-chrome steel, which outline the rows of windows, glistening in the sun and charging its elegant stone surfaces with life. Slightly thicker middle runs, terminating in splayed seashell forms catch bursts of light at the end of each setback, exaggerating the long, steep pull of the building's lines.

Debate has been lively about the McGraw-Hill Building, designed by Raymond Hood. Some would categorize it as Art Deco for its signage, detailing, and use of color. Others argue that it is an International-Style building (and, therefore, avant-garde) for the regularity of its cladding, which conforms to the steel frame underneath, and for its emphatic horizontal lines.

PAGES 58-59: Looking southwest across the Central Park boat pond toward Central Park West.
PRECEDING PAGES: Manhattan seen from Brooklyn, slightly north of the Brooklyn Bridge.
OVERLEAF, LEFT: Riverside Church on Riverside Drive between West 120th and West 122nd streets, built by Allen and Collens, Henry C. Pelton and Burnham Hoyt in 1930, with a south wing added by Collens, Willis and Beckonert in 1960.
OVERLEAF, RIGHT: The Cooper Union Foundation Building on East 7th Street between Cooper Square and Third Avenue. by Frederick A. Peterson, 1859; it was reconstructed by John Hejduk in 1974.

In daylight, the airiness of the blue-green terra-cotta walls is unmistakable and dramatic—the great volume of interior space enclosed only by a thin layer of protection against the weather. Seen this way, the building's Modernist credentials are clear.

Sufficiently admired by Philip Johnson and Henry-Russell Hitchcock to be included in the 1932 show that they organized at The Museum of Modern Art, "Modern Architecture: International Exhibition," the McGraw-Hill Building also was one of just six American buildings—and the only Manhattan building—to be included in their watershed book of the same year, *The International Style: Architecture since 1922.* In retrospect, the choice seems obvious, since in its appearance of near-weightlessness it has hardly been surpassed by any tall building in Manhattan.

The black-and-white stone top of the Fuller Building, worked in zigs and zags almost like a textile, seems to pull the whole structure together neatly, rather than letting it dissolve into the sky. At Rockefeller Center, that (not entirely unsuccessful) experiment in urbanism-for-profit, gilded and polychrome panels mark the entrances to individual buildings, enlivening the otherwise stark shapes and giving them human dimension.

Layers of time are apparent here as well, not in great stretches, as in other cities, but most often, just in spots. An eccentric mid-nineteenth-century wooden pier structure at Manhattan's tip, for example, is left over from a once flourishing maritime economy; small, simple wooden houses with porches, dating from about the same time, survive on the densely populated Upper East Side as evidence of a once near-rural ecology.

The nation's largest city also continues to be governed from a small but elegantly proportioned palacelike City Hall that was completed in 1811 and sits

LEFT: **The Bennett Building at 99 Nassau Street between Fulton and Ann, built by Arthur D. Gilman in 1873.**
OVERLEAF, LEFT: **A statue of Puck overlooks East Houston Street from its northeastern corner of the Puck Building, 295–309 Lafayette Street, Albert Wagner, architect, 1885 and 1892.**
OVERLEAF, RIGHT: **The shuttered south wall of the Puck Building.**

in a little park in lower Manhattan—now ringed by skyscrapers. Not too far away, the largest and most impressive group of nineteenth-century cast-iron buildings in the world can be found. A great step forward in terms of economy and efficiency, their prefabricated metal parts held large panes of glass that allowed ample daylight to enter the buildings.

Most famous among them, the Haughwout Building also happened to be the first commercial building to be fitted with an Otis elevator. It is still admired for the grace and proportions of the columns and arches that are repeated in rows across its façade. Although its appearance obviously is based on a historic model, its metal-and-glass walls and the easy means of vertical access within were elements that would lead, within a few decades, to the development of the skyscraper.

It would take a while, though, for mass-produced elements to dominate the façades of buildings and for the machine aesthetic to prevail. In fact, on buildings constructed up until nearly the mid-twentieth century (when ornament was firmly banished for philosophical reasons and also ceased to make sense, considering the scale and materials of new buildings) one can find, at virtually every level, statues, sculptures, and carvings that, although created in the midst of a constant rush for profit, suggest an atmosphere in which time and money would have been no object.

Aggressive and benign figures—animal, human, mythic, symbolic—can be found engaged in what appear to be acts of holding up or reclining against cornices, lintels, columns, and clocks and gesturing, smiling, or scowling from within pediments, niches, and corner reveals.

Well-known artists (such as Elie Nadelman and Daniel Chester French) have been among the contributors, but more often, the work has been done anonymously. Some of it is integral to the composition and rhythm of the building (notably Mercury poised gallantly above Hercules and Minerva

RIGHT: The cast-iron E. V. Haughwout Building at 488 Broadway and Broome Street, by the architect J. P. Gaynor, completed in 1859. The building's four upper floors are lit by a total of 92 windows.

at the entrance to Grand Central Station—a dynamic configuration that, although pretty much hemmed in by skyscrapers now, can still be seen silhouetted against the sky from some vantage points). Others serve more as evidence of a human touch and the sheer joy of embellishment. All, however, enoble the activities that take place around them.

Nor is the whole necessarily greater than the sum of its parts. Despite everything working against them in this dense, complicated, and gridded urban environment, a surprising number of the twentieth century's most important and influential architects have managed to build in Manhattan—and, in fact, to build some of the pivotal buildings of their careers.

Louis Sullivan, for example, this country's first "modern" architect, whose career spanned the late nineteenth and early twentieth centuries and who practiced almost exclusively in Chicago and the Midwest, did design one building in Manhattan. Completed in 1898, the Bayard-Condict Building on Bleecker Street turned out to be Manhattan's first truly modern skyscraper as well as one of the finest works of Louis Sullivan's alternately brilliant and tragic career.

One of the earliest of the "tall buildings," which, by then, had become technically possible (although by today's standards, it can be hard to see why a 12-story building would have been impressive), the Bayard-Condict was also the first tall building in Manhattan to actually look like what it was. Not designed to resemble the masonry structures of the past either in the way it was shaped or the way it was clad, and not designed in imitation of any historical style (as other tall buildings were at the time), the Bayard-Condict was, instead, fitted with a façade of pale, delicate hand-molded terra cotta that lightly covered its steel frame.

The long smooth vertical lines of terra cotta rise straight up, past the identical rows of offices, to a series of graceful arches—and, above those, six angels, whose wings are spread as if ready for flight. The appearance of lightness and the emphasis on the vertical were breathtakingly new; the richly complex ornament that Sullivan designed for the spandrel panels and the crown above the entrance were original, abstract, and based upon forms found in nature. And Louis Sullivan (who would soon die in poverty and obscurity) was heralded as the architect who had solved the (aesthetic) problem of what to do with the skyscraper.

Just four years after that building's completion, one of Sullivan's best-known fellow Chicagoans and contemporaries, Daniel H. Burnham, brought his only Manhattan building to completion as well. Known colloquially from then until now as the Flatiron Building, it earned its name because of the architectural solution that Burnham devised for a weird, "skinny" site—that is, a shape that was thought to resemble the implement that laundresses used to iron clothing.

Burnham had taken the masonry building pretty much to its limit in 1891 with his 16-story Monadnock Building in Chicago, which had load-bearing walls, madly thick at the base to support all the weight and small, deep windows tunneled into those walls. He also had been chief architect of Chicago's 1893 World's Columbian Exposition, which Louis Sullivan had derided as a calamity for American architecture because of its emphasis on looking backward to Classical and Renaissance forms (except for his own famous Transportation Building, that is). But in Manhattan, the 22-story steel-framed Flatiron Building that Daniel Burnham designed was, in its way, an expression of new possibilities.

Although its rusticated limestone cladding and French Renaissance motif were somewhat recidivist, its straight-up straight-ahead posture was not. Slicing the air as if to move through it, the building's thinnest edge is thin enough to seem a bit unreal, even mysterious. And in its slenderness, the Flatiron Building presaged shapes that were to come.

Manhattan is also home to two of the most important glass towers of our

OVERLEAF, LEFT: **A Brooklyn view of Manhattan: the Empire State Building, framed in an arch of the Manhattan Bridge.**
OVERLEAF, RIGHT: **On the George Washington Bridge, looking west toward New Jersey.**

time. The first, Lever House, designed by Gordon Bunshaft of Skidmore, Owings and Merrill for the soap company that produced Lifebuoy and Tide, and completed in 1952, initiated the use of a nearly all-glass façade for a tall office building. Mr. Bunshaft also set a precedent by raising the office floors above the streets, foregoing a lobby or shops, and giving the ground floor over to open space and public use. (The company, which had been founded in the United Kingdom, had, in fact, been at the forefront of architecture and design since the nineteenth century. In 1888, Lord Leverhulme hired the architect William Owen to design a company town, Port Sunlight, near Liverpool, which emphasized tranquility, nature, order, hygiene, efficiency, and excellence in design—and which was one of the earliest and most influential forerunners of the English "garden city.")

Sparkling in the sun, the green glass and stainless-steel building is set like two prisms: the lower one, a slim horizontal parallel to Park Avenue; the upper one, a slim vertical perpendicular to the street. Modestly—or extravagantly— the composition takes up far less of the site than it could have. A slight separation between the two forms also gives the tower the appearance of almost floating in space. The building's critical success was an indication to corporate America that avant-garde theory could be adapted to its needs. With its clean lines and sleek surfaces, Lever House became an international symbol of a new age.

It was Mies van der Rohe, however, the great German-born architect who lived, taught, and practiced in Chicago for many years, who generally is credited with having had the greatest influence on postwar office design in the United States (not necessarily a compliment, since his pristine glass-and-steel aesthetic often was badly imitated—the result being drab, stark boxes). The first office tower that he ever built was in Manhattan: the Seagram Building, completed in 1958, when he was already in his seventies.

A tall bronze and brown glass tower that rises straight up in a large, open plaza, the Seagram Building is an advertisement for Modernist theory and vocabulary. Although Mies was accused of severity and blamed for other people's empty work, this subtle and elegant structure demonstrates his extreme care with the physical and tactile elements of architecture, in addition to the visual, and his ability to fuse timeless properties of Classical architecture with new materials and technology.

Mies believed that the proportions of a building were crucial and that they had to be sensed more than calculated. And his genius at doing just that is obvious as one walks up the three shallow steps from the street and across the wide granite-paved plaza toward the powerfully symmetrical building and into its high glass-walled lobby.

Inside, Mies's sensuous use of materials and his insistence on fastidious craftsmanship are obvious as well: Travertine, bronze, and glass mosaic are used simply but with full exploitation of their textures and colors. The lobby's glass walls frame careful views of the street and of other buildings, creating a distinctive combination of openness and urbanism. Abstract from a distance, the Seagram Building is, close up, as glamorous an office building as any that came before it.

Another twentieth-century master, and this country's greatest architect, Frank Lloyd Wright, also managed, somehow, to build one building in Manhattan. Completed in 1959, just after Wright's death, the Guggenheim Museum on Fifth Avenue was a late architectural tour de force in a career that had produced a great many. The Guggenheim is an extremely subjective work, representative of no particular style: From the outside, it is a combination of horizontals and spheres, the most significant of which is a gravity-

OVERLEAF, LEFT: **The Cary Building, 105–107 Chambers Street, by Gamaliel King and John Kellum, 1857. Its cast-iron façade (cast by Daniel Badger's Architectural Iron Works) is painted to look like stone.**
OVERLEAF, RIGHT: **The Hearst Magazine Building, 959 Eighth Avenue, by Joseph Urban, 1928.**
FOLLOWING PAGES, LEFT: **Marbled and tiled ceiling of the Film Center Building at 630 Ninth Avenue, Buchman and Kahn, architects, 1929.**
FOLLOWING PAGES, RIGHT: *The Parrot Girl,* **one of the Howard Chandler Christy murals in Café des Artistes at 1 West 67th Street, painted in 1932.**

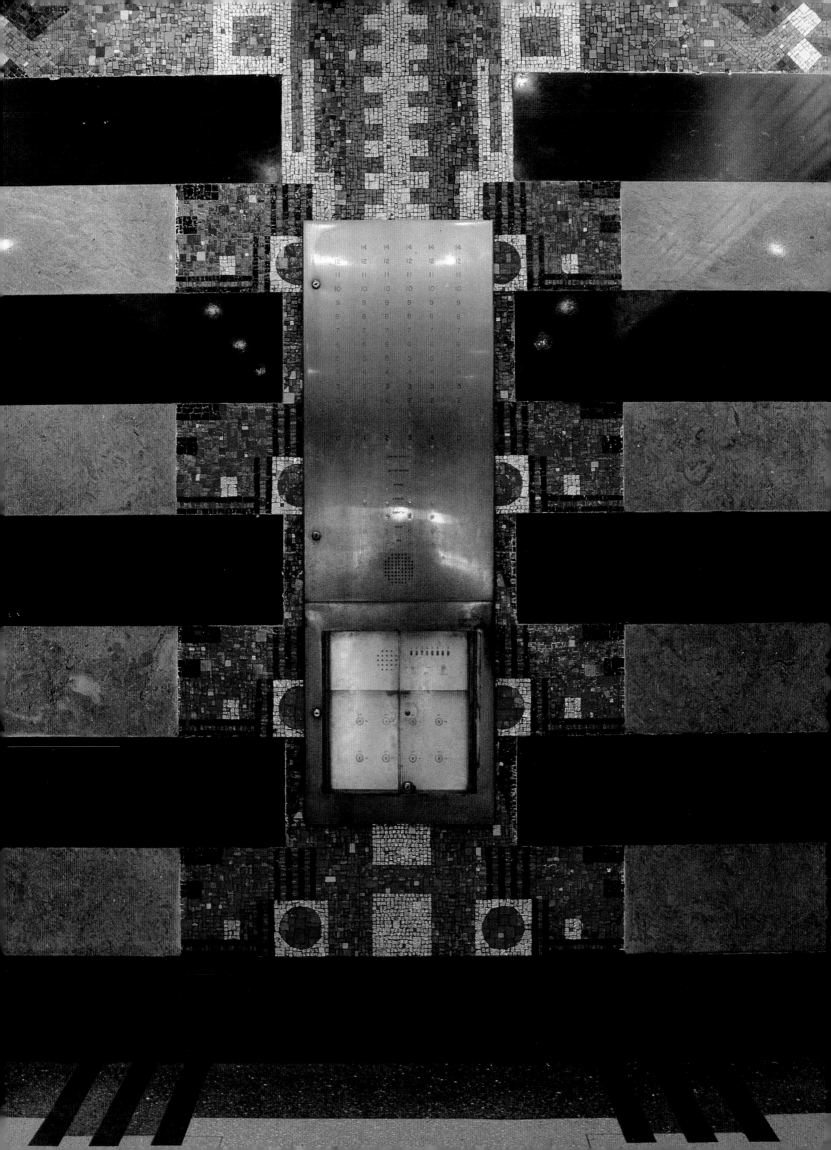

defying upside-down spiral set on a slight diagonal; inside, the composition depends almost entirely upon space and light for its extraordinary effect.

A low-ceilinged entrance makes the full-height, glass-domed central space seem especially dramatic. And the long spiral ramp that threads around the space and leads visitors from the top down creates a mesmerizing human promenade that becomes an integral part of the experience.

The building was controversial from the beginning, however. Frank Lloyd Wright had difficulty getting the unusual structure through the city's building regulations (although by that time he probably had gotten used to such problems, since consultants and civil authorities were continually telling him that his designs were unbuildable). Besides that, a group of eminent visual artists of the day petitioned against the building's construction.

The tilt of the ramp and its banked edges can, in fact, be problematic—forcing the visitor to tilt, for one thing. On the other hand, the museum is organized so that orientation is simple and immediate, which is no small virtue for an art museum. And when an exhibition does happen to "work" in this environment, there is reason for exultation.

The Guggenheim is an alluring presence from the street: Small spans of glass offer a hint of what is going on inside and the provocative shapes exert a strong pull on passersby. At night, the museum is at its most beautiful, when the weathering of its concrete exterior is camouflaged and it appears to be an exercise in pure form, weightless, and striped and glowing with light—as in one of Frank Lloyd Wright's nighttime renderings.

Not entirely dissimilar (although nothing is quite like the work of Frank Lloyd Wright), the Whitney Museum of American Art on Madison Avenue,

PRECEDING PAGES, LEFT: Engine Company 55, at 363 Broome Street, built by R. H. Robertson in 1898.

PRECEDING PAGES, RIGHT: Entrance to the Cooper-Hewitt Museum, which holds the decorative arts collection amassed by the Cooper and Hewitt families.

RIGHT: The entrance of the City Center Fifty-Fifth Street Theater on West 55th Street, formerly a temple for the Ancient and Accepted Order of the Mystic Shrine.

which was designed by Marcel Breuer in the 1960s, has an upside-down look and one of the most enticing of art museum entrances.

A stepped and inverted form, the Whitney is both an idiosyncratic structure and an eloquent example of the thicker, rougher, darker buildings that were designed in great numbers after the heyday of light steel-and-glass buildings. It also is probably the finest work of Marcel Breuer, who had been a student and faculty member at the Bauhaus in Germany before coming to the United States to teach at Harvard and practice with Walter Gropius.

The Whitney, while certainly tactile, is not quite as rough as some of its peers. Its cladding, in fact, is of a rather elegant gray granite. There is some lightness, too, in the canopied, moatlike entrance that leads to the glass-walled lobby. And the way that the entrance stretches out to the street with the museum interior revealed behind establishes a subtle but powerful lure. It can be difficult to walk by the Whitney Museum without peeking in.

Despite how strange both the Guggenheim and the Whitney may have seemed when they were first built, each one now looks as though it belongs exactly where it is.

Manhattan continues to be a fertile ground for new architecture. In 1977, Hugh Stubbins's Citicorp Center rose in a great diagonal slice through the sky, challenging the flat roofs of Modernism. In the 1980s, the Minimalist aesthetics of architects such as I. M. Pei and Cesar Pelli have appeared in jazzed-up versions. From the office of the former, for example, has come a huge, faceted, dark-glass convention center; from the latter, the taut multicolored glass tower over the now nearly unrecognizable Museum of Modern

RIGHT: The Pythian Temple at 135 West 70th Street was built in 1927 as a Masonic lodge, and reflects its architect's penchant for schematic building. Thomas W. Lamb, known for his great movie palaces, adorned this 9-story structure with a range of Sumerian and Egyptian motifs, including Pharoahlike figures seated on the roof. Pictured, a detail of the Doric columns and polychromatic panels along the base of the building, which now belongs to the City University of New York.
OVERLEAF, LEFT: The glossy setbacks of Trump Tower at 725 Fifth Avenue, Der Scutt, architect, 1983.
OVERLEAF, RIGHT: A tower of Cesar Pelli's World Financial Center at Battery Park, with the wavy reflection of Cass Gilbert's 90 West Street in its windows.

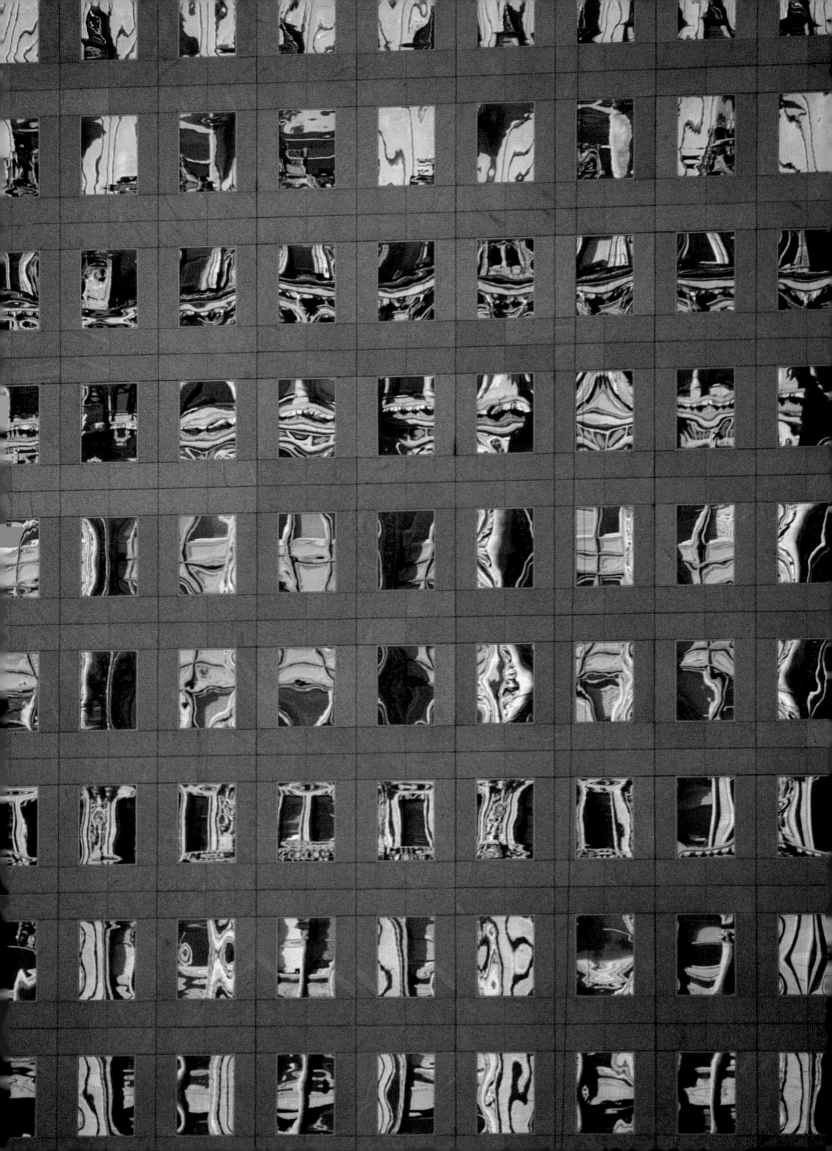

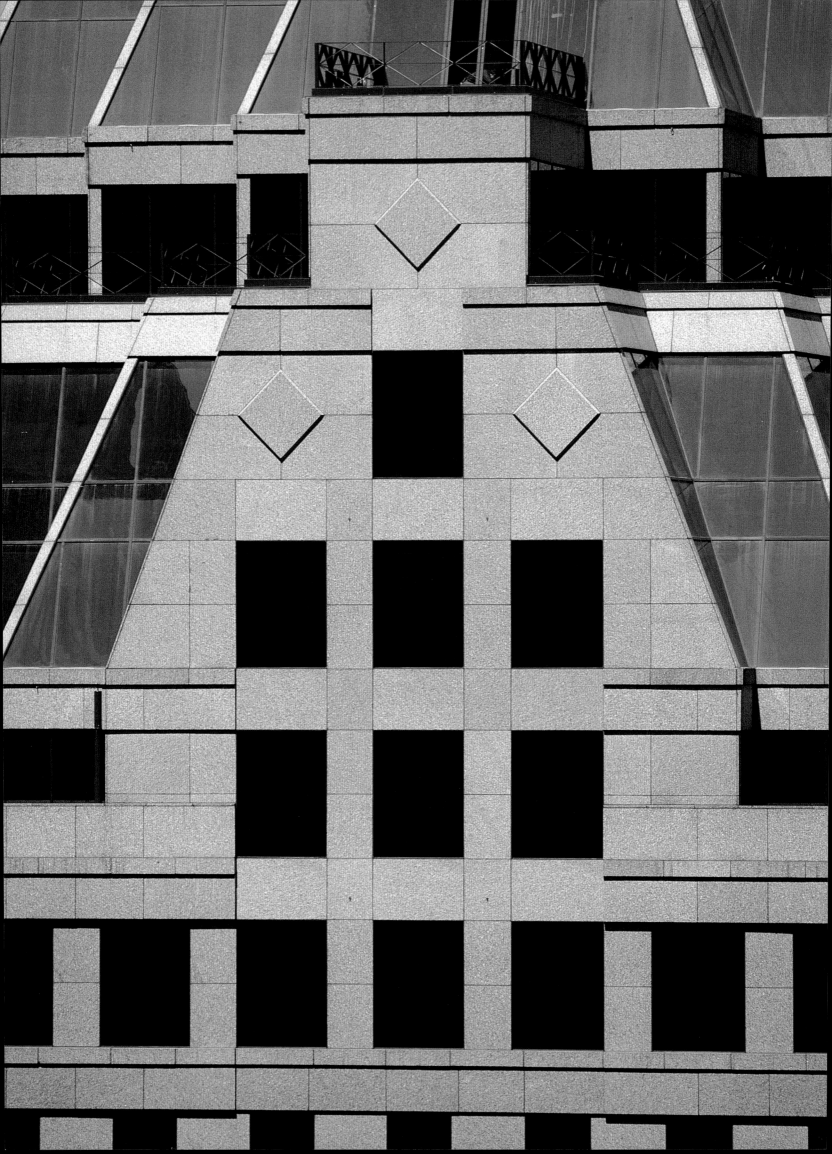

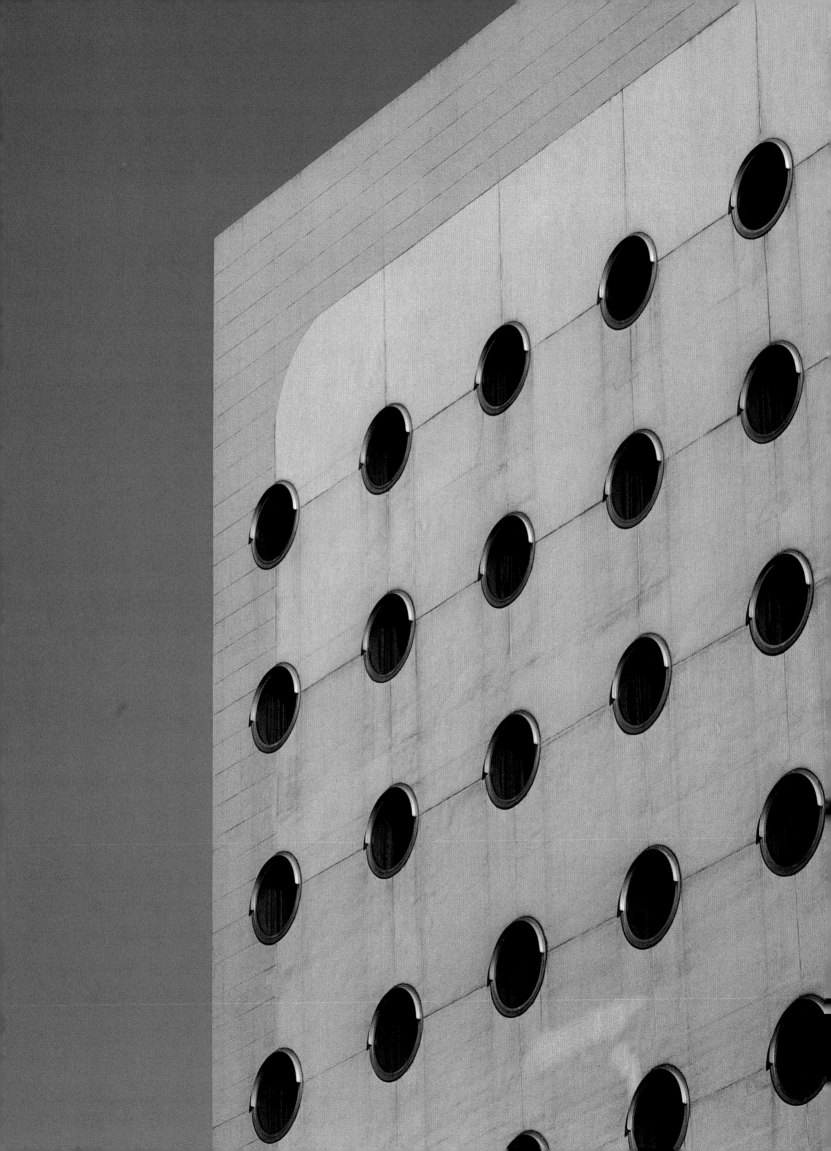

Art, as well as a cluster of equally taut masonry-and-glass towers that rim the edge of lower Manhattan.

The historical borrowings that have come to be referred to as Postmodernist are represented in Manhattan as well—starting, more or less, with the work of Philip Johnson. Mr. Johnson had, years before, worked with Mies van der Rohe on the Seagram Building, and had designed the very Miesian sculpture court at The Museum of Modern Art and the glassy former home of the Asia Society, but in 1984, he completed the AT&T Building on Madison Avenue, which sent an enormous, classically derived broken pediment into the skyline.

There have been more pediments since then, as well as a variation on a mansard roof, and some grudging little triangles and domes that finish off ponderous buildings that, more often than not, come thundering to the ground. The posh materials and attention to detail that characterized earlier buildings in Manhattan tend to be missing from these new models, which generally are playing to the grandstand. And urban considerations often have been pushed aside.

These buildings are not the whole story, though, and the tenets of Modernism continue to be influential. The same architect, in fact, who designed the ungainly Equitable Building almost simultaneously designed an urbane glass tower with a clear and elegant all-glass entrance, just across town. New work is surfacing as well, from younger architects and architects from elsewhere—who are, as in the past, drawn to this place. Which means that, at least for the foreseeable future, Manhattan will continue to serve as a sign of the times.

—Ellen Posner

PRECEDING PAGES, LEFT: The 1987 E. F. Hutton Building, by Roche, Dinkeloo and Associates, 31 West 52nd Street, covered in Finnish coral granite.

PRECEDING PAGES, RIGHT: The former National Maritime Union Building is now named the Edward and Theresa O'Toole Building and belongs to St. Vincent's Hospital (36 Seventh Avenue, Albert C. Ledner, architect, 1964).

RIGHT: The view east from 57th Street and Sixth Avenue finds the Crown Building in front of IBM, left, Trump Tower, center, and AT&T's granite World Headquarters, right.

PAGE 95: The Central Park West skyline, looking northwest from Central Park at the vicinity of 74th Street.

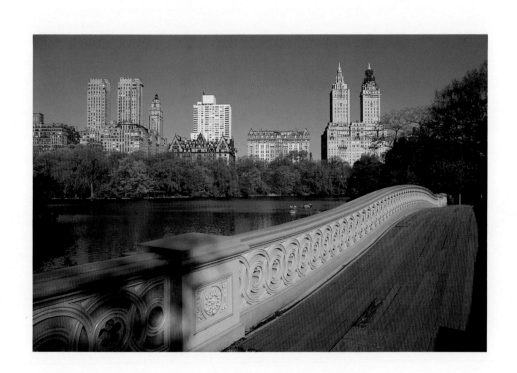

THE WORLD TRADE CENTER

Whether from the neighboring boroughs, from across the expansive plaza, or from within the cyclopean lobby, a view of the World Trade Center is an invitation that beckons the imagination to soar. This 1970s icon to height, by architects Minoru Yamasaki and Emery Roth, towers above the original monoliths that first made the dark canyons of Wall Street famous.

The Gothic arches in the lobbies, at the bases and the tops of the twin towers, not only echo the surrounding Gothic Revival forms of Trinity Church, the Trinity Building, the Woolworth Building, and the West Street Building but also reinforce the analogy of the modern skyscraper in America to the great Gothic cathedrals of medieval France.

THIS PAGE, TOP:
On the left, the North Tower and on the right, the Vista International Hotel, each part of the World Trade Center.

ABOVE, LEFT:
The South Tower, foreground, and the North Tower, bottom right.

ABOVE, RIGHT:
Viewing the World Trade Center from across the Hudson River, in New Jersey.

OPPOSITE:
The view from Brooklyn, looking west.

OVERLEAF:
The World Trade Center's North Tower, top, with the Vista Hotel on the bottom at the right and the South Tower on its left.

THE CON-ED BUILDING

The 23-story office tower, built by Warren and Wetmore in 1926 for Consolidated Edison, is floors above the previous decade's Italian palazzo headquarters built by Henry J. Hardenbergh. Made of limestone, the tower is surmounted by a colonnaded temple, which is capped by an 8-foot-high lantern fashioned in the style of an ancient urn. The ensemble, located at 14th Street and Irving Place and punctuated with torches as symbols of immortality, constitutes a memorial to the Consolidated Edison employees who died in World War I. At night, special lighting within the lantern and behind the colonnade lends a unique distinction to the building's crown.

RIGHT:
The clock on Warren and Wetmore's Consolidated Edison Company tower of 1926 faces west, looking out over Irving Place, and marks the transition from office space to colonnaded temple.

OVERLEAF, LEFT:
A symbol of immortality, the torch on the Consolidated Edison tower serves as a memorial to the employees who died in World War I.

OVERLEAF, RIGHT:
At the pinnacle of Consolidated Edison's 23-story tower is an 8-foot-high lantern.

THE JAVITS CENTER

Partner-in-charge James Ingo Freed's idea for the Jacob A. Javits Convention Center, built by I. M. Pei and Partners and stretching from West 34th to West 39th streets between Eleventh and Twelfth avenues, was sparked by England's Crystal Palace and Paris's Grand Palais. The structure provides its visitors with a sweeping panorama of the Manhattan skyline as viewed through Freed's grand ferrovitreous grid. Completed in 1987, the Convention Center encompasses a 60,000-foot-square public galleria overlooking an exhibition hall, on the upper level, which culminates in a pavilion overlooking the Hudson. The views, varied and spectacular, offer an enhanced sense of New York.

THIS PAGE, TOP:
The 5-block-long Convention Center, standing between Eleventh and Twelfth avenues: view from Twelfth Avenue.

THIS PAGE, BOTTOM:
The east façade.

RIGHT:
The west façade.

OVERLEAF:
Designer James Ingo Freed conceived of the Convention Center in part as a Manhattan version of Paris's Grand Palais.

FOLLOWING PAGES:
The interior of the Convention Center, facing east into Manhattan, at dusk.

THE EQUITABLE LIFE ASSURANCE SOCIETY BUILDING

The Equitable Life Assurance Society's 3-tiered office tower is clad in limestone, granite, and glass. It rises 54 stories from the east side of Seventh Avenue between West 51st and West 52nd streets and is capped with arched windows 53 feet high, a crowning motif that echoes the tower's main entrance below. Designed by Edward Larrabee Barnes and Associates and opened in 1987, the Equitable Building is connected to the PaineWebber Building, on the same block, and to Rockefeller Center to the east by an underground corridor.

Inside, monumental murals by Roy Lichtenstein, Sol LeWitt, and Sandro Chia, sculpture by Paul Manship, and the famous Thomas Hart Benton work, *America Today,* have been incorporated into the tower's design. The Whitney Museum of American Art maintains two exhibition spaces in the tower and an ample galleria, connecting West 51st and West 52nd streets at midblock, which includes a sculpture by Barry Flannagan.

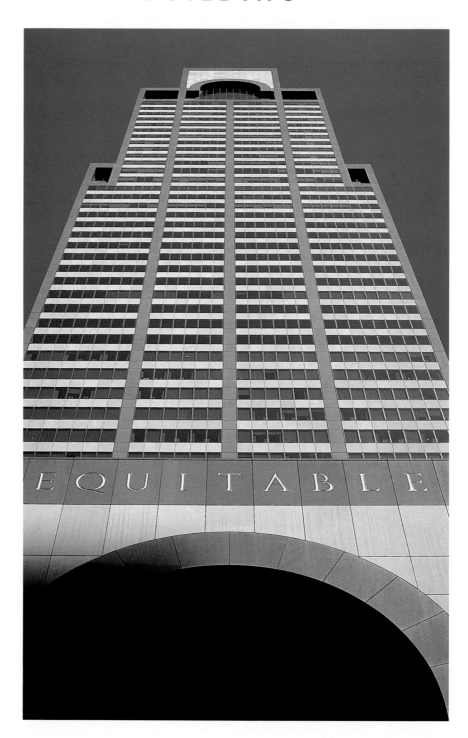

THIS PAGE:
The limestone, granite, and glass façade.

RIGHT:
Equitable's interior includes *Mural with Blue Brushstroke* by Roy Lichtenstein.

THE FLATIRON BUILDING

Like a beautifully crafted book standing open, the curve of its narrow binding exposed, the Fuller Building is picturesquely sited on a wedge-shaped island between Fifth Avenue and Broadway, its elegant spine facing 23rd Street.

Clad in decorative terra cotta, the 23-story skyscraper caught the public's imagination right from the time it was erected in 1903. Its unusual shape earned it the nickname the Flatiron Building, even though its plan is in actuality a right triangle, not shaped like a flatiron at all, and its Broadway and Fifth Avenue façades are unequal in length.

Architect D. H. Burnham's elegant design and fortuitous siting across the street from historic and scenic Madison Square Park have attracted many artists to capture its changing silhouette and complexion at all seasons of the year, and at almost every time of day. The famous photographs of the building by Alfred Stieglitz and Edward Steichen have contributed to making the Flatiron Building the skyscraper *par excellence* at the turn of the century.

RIGHT:
175 Fifth Avenue, originally intended to be known as the Fuller Building, points due north, although the street grid is crooked.

THE FORD FOUNDATION

The offices of the Ford Foundation, designed by Roche,
Dinkeloo and Associates in
1967, overlook an indoor
garden that is enclosed in glass,
Cor Ten steel, and masonry. A
thematic descendant of the
eighteenth- and nineteenth-century Anglo-Chinois garden and
of the Victorian conservatory,
the Ford Foundation garden
serves as an extension of the
park setting of adjacent Tudor
City, a domestic enclave that
rises above the traffic and din of
East 42nd Street between First
and Second avenues.

TENEMENTS

New York City's northward expansion in the early nineteenth century left many houses of wealthy families, seeking their privacy farther uptown, to be subdivided into multiple-family dwellings. The practice of subdivision continued into the twentieth century, although some older neighborhoods, such as Chelsea and the Charlton-King-Vandam Historic District, managed to maintain single-owner residences.

With the 1830s came the building of tenements, which could house more people at a better profit, though by 1879 conditions such as overcrowding and substandard lighting and ventilation systems prompted the Tenement Law.

Richard Morris Hunt, who was the first American architect to be educated at the Ecole des Beaux Arts in Paris, established the modern apartment house in New York with his Stuyvesant Apartments, 1869–1870, at 142 East 18th Street near Irving Place, and apartment-house living was here to stay.

Improved tenements and modern apartments did not displace inadequate housing; crowded conditions still prevail throughout the city.

The district of SoHo, which stands for "South of Houston," represents a unique example of conversion. During the 1950s, 1960s, and 1970s, artists gradually converted early-nineteenth-century row houses, mid- to late-nineteenth-century warehouses, and cast-iron emporiums into lofts where they could work and live economically. But the subsequent gentrification has attracted high-income tenants in the past decade, along with fashionable shops and boutiques, restaurants, and galleries.

LEFT, TOP:
Doorway with pediment, 420 Broome Street.

LEFT, BOTTOM:
191 Ninth Avenue.

THIS PAGE:
Harlem, viewed from Morningside Drive, looking northeast.

OVERLEAF, LEFT:
Apartment house entrance, Chinatown.

OVERLEAF, RIGHT:
The Vesuvio Bakery at 160 Prince Street.

FOLLOWING PAGES:
Detail of an old SoHo exterior.

BRIDGES

The island of Manhattan is linked to New Jersey as well as its surrounding boroughs by bridges, which range in span from 300 feet (the Third Avenue, Madison Avenue, and 145th Street bridges) to 3,500 feet (the George Washington Bridge). Most of Manhattan's bridges are suspension bridges, with the notable exception of the cantilevered Queensboro Bridge, which joins Manhattan with Queens. In principle, the Queensboro Bridge's horizontal structure is supported by the downward force behind a fulcrum and the towers on either side. These account at least in part for the visual interruptions along the staccato drape of the steel trusswork. The Queensboro Bridge, long in coming, was initially designed in 1868 and finished in 1909. Within this time span Queens joined Greater New York (1898), money was appropriated for designs that were then changed, and the project's original name, Blackwell's Island Bridge, was abandoned in favor of its present title. Austrian-born Gustav Lindenthal, the celebrated engineer, and architect Henry Hornbostel were in charge of the undertaking's completion.

 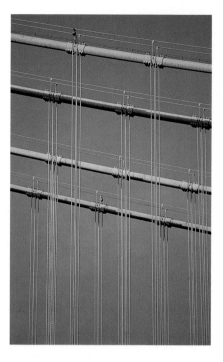

ABOVE, LEFT:
The top of the eastern tower of engineer Gustav Lindenthal's and architects Palmer and Hornbostel's Queensboro Bridge, east of Second Avenue at 59th Street, opened for traffic in 1909.

ABOVE, RIGHT:
Steel suspension cables on the Manhattan Bridge. It was redesigned three times in nine years to satisfy a succession of municipal chief engineers.

RIGHT:
Approaching Manhattan through the Gothic towers of the Brooklyn Bridge of 1883, designed and constructed by John A. Roebling; after an accident on the site with fatal consequences, the work was completed by his son and chief engineer Washington Roebling and daughter-in-law Emily.

OVERLEAF:
The Brooklyn Bridge with lower Manhattan in the background. Its roadbed and floor are composed entirely of steel, an engineering first for bridges this large.

FOLLOWING PAGES:
The Brooklyn Bridge's stability is due in part to hundreds of cable stays fanning out from the granite towers.

At first many New Yorkers disliked the appearance of the bridge, though they eventually came to respect it, with its superstructure a webwork of interlaced steel, and its piers of medievallike granite. The finials on top of the bridge's four steel towers came into acceptance as well, deemed appropriate crowns, shaped like the queen in chess. Even the Great Gatsby, author Sharon Reier has noted, admired the Queensboro Bridge as Long Island's link to Manhattan.

The Manhattan Bridge, also completed in 1909, was fraught with its own controversy. Lindenthal, for example, not only proposed seemingly radical innovations in the design of the suspension bridge but also outlined a plan to accommodate large assembly halls in the bridge's anchorages, which sparked prolonged debate and never received approval.

The grand entrance to the bridge, at Canal Street and the Bowery, was created by the Beaux-Arts architects Carrère and Hastings. To give the entrance a flourish, they borrowed from the triumphal Porte St. Denis gateway in Paris and the curved colonnade (by Gianlorenzo Bernini) that encloses the piazza of St. Peter's in Rome. Over the entrance's coffered arch, an animated relief by Charles Rumsey, the *Buffalo Hunt,* provides the complex with an American signature.

The Triborough Bridge, connecting the three boroughs of Manhattan, the Bronx, and Queens, was completed in 1936 after more than twenty years of discussion. The northward growth of Manhattan prompted a continuous lobby by the business communities of Harlem, Queens, and the Bronx for a bridge at 125th Street, to be a much-needed alternative to the Queensboro Bridge. The unique genius of Robert Moses finally brought one about, and in the process the Triborough Bridge Authority has since become a model for all the city's major bridges.

An icon to progress, John A. Roebling's Brooklyn Bridge has inspired countless artists. Its innovative spun-steel cables, strung like flaxen strands from two massive Gothic arches, evoked from poet Hart Crane the aspiration "O Harp and Altar," which was the theme of his last epic work. The bridge, uniting Manhattan and Brooklyn, is considered an engineering classic, in which modern cable technology is supported by traditional architectural form.

RIGHT:
Brooklyn view of the Manhattan Bridge.
OVERLEAF:
The graceful structure of the 1,380-foot-span Triborough Bridge, seen at sunrise from Manhattan.
FOLLOWING PAGES:
The four-towered Queensboro Bridge, a cantilevered anomaly among Manhattan's sleek suspension bridges.

GLASS TOWERS

Park Avenue was virtually an unbroken, double row of limestone and brick—the solid, secure materials of the early twentieth century. Then Lever House was completed in 1952, redefining the aesthetic of the company headquarters into something shiny and new. The blue-green glass tower broke the matte line of its neighbors with light, reflection, and space. Set to one side of a low, horizontal slab, it provides the site with a sense of airiness. Its translucent windows are offset by darker, opaque spandrels and all is contained in a lively grid of stainless steel. The grid also forms the track for the building's own motorized, window-cleaning gondola—an innovative solution to the problem of cleaning windows that do not open.

The modern, urban symbol of the gleaming skylines also owes much to the vision of Mies van der Rohe, whose sheer, unadorned towers were often accused of being so austere they were unfriendly. His Seagram Building of 1959—a nearly 500-foot-high shaft of bronze and amber glass rising from square column supports—proved such accusations wrong. Instead of

building a setback tower over a base that skims the sidewalk, the architect set the entire structure back on a generous, open plaza. Seagram's interior appointments are just as hospitable: floor-to-ceiling doors, custom aluminum and stainless-steel hardware, and even custom lettering on the mailboxes set the standard for postwar, commercial luxury. Overzealous city zoning boards revised the city codes in 1961 to encourage such designs, but this only helped to wreak havoc on Manhattan's sense of order by prompting much cheaper imitations.

THIS PAGE:

The Seagram Building at 375 Park Avenue from 52nd to 53rd streets was built by Mies van der Rohe and Philip Johnson, and completed in 1958. Beneath its calm and shiny exterior is a complicated network of supports, though the public plaza below is a genuinely tranquil space.

RIGHT:

Lever House, a glass-and-stone tower at 390 Park Avenue, completed in 1952 by Gordon Bunshaft of Skidmore, Owings and Merrill; this was Bunshaft's first major building. Its sacrifice of commercial space for the sake of air, space, and circulation was a revelation in the annals of urban skyscraper design.

ENCLAVES

A stage set, a mews, and stables produced three of Manhattan's most arresting residential enclaves. Pomander Walk, a double row of late-medieval-style English manor houses running from West 94th to West 95th streets between Broadway and West End Avenue, was built in 1921 by King and Campbell. The small grouping features characteristic half-timbering, square-headed windows, brick-work, fieldstone, and high gables. The street and its name were inspired by the stage sets for *Pomander Walk,* a play produced in New York City and London that was named after its setting, a tiny street in the London suburb of Chiswick.

Washington Mews is a secluded lane flanked by early- to late-nineteenth-century stables converted to residential use. It extends from Fifth Avenue to University Place behind Washington Square North's row houses in Greenwich Village. *Mews* is a British term used to describe a stables and service area and is used here to designate one of Manhattan's most charming enclaves.

Sniffen Court on the south side of 36th Street between Lexington and Third avenues was named for John Sniffen, who built this double row of brick stables in the 1850s. Although the stables have been substantially altered in their conversion to residential use, the scale has changed little, and enough brickwork survives to provide the enclave with authentic character. The façade of sculptor Malvina Hoffman's former studio stands at the end of the alley, and a replica of a frieze of horsemen from the Parthenon overlooks the stable's old well.

THE WOOLWORTH BUILDING

In his world-famous Woolworth Building, architect Cass Gilbert succeeded in uniting the respected traditions of architecture and decoration with modern technology. Completed in 1913 and standing at 233 Broadway, the building, with its brilliant combination of Gothic decorations, flying buttresses, terra-cotta cladding, and a steel skeleton, was christened the Cathedral of Commerce. For almost two decades it remained the tallest and most revered skyscraper in the world.

The dome with merging pendentives, and the decoration of the building's lobby were inspired in part by the mausoleum of Galla Placidia in Ravenna, Italy—a unique jewel of early Christian mosaic work. Gilbert's gods of commerce are depicted in brilliant color, presiding over the great hall. His Gothic tower celebrates the modern transubstantiation of iron and clay into the building's skeleton and surface.

Surrounding the skylight, which illuminates the staircase from lobby to mezzanine, is a complexity of colorful figures, combining whimsical aspects of the retail trade with significant dates in the company's international expansion.

THIS PAGE, TOP:
The lobby mosaic depicts the gods of commerce.

BOTTOM:
The building's lobby ceiling contains a compass in the apex of its mosaic dome that points due north.

RIGHT:
The Woolworth tower soars upward from the 29th floor, is inset on all four sides at the 42nd, changes from square to octagonal at the 48th, and becomes a 3-story, 125-foot-high roof at the 52nd.

OVERLEAF:
Surrounding the illuminated stained-glass ceiling are caricatures of retail business figures, and the coats of arms of affiliated countries.

ALWYN COURT

Named for Alwyn Ball, Jr., an owner of the construction company that built it in 1909, Alwyn Court at West 58th Street and Seventh Avenue is one of the most elegant apartment residences erected at the turn of the century. While the interiors were stripped and altered, and its main entrance was moved from its original spot in the rounded corner bay during 1930s changes, the exterior remains intact. The rich François I decoration that lays like lace over the façade is remarkably well preserved. During Alwyn Court's most recent renovation, mural painter Richard Haas reproduced the terra-cotta reliefs for part of the decoration of one of the apartments and designed a trompe l'oeil architectural mural for the building's atrium, which was created by enclosing the airshaft.

THIS PAGE, LEFT:
The original entrance to the Alwyn Court apartment house on the northeast corner at 58th Street and Seventh Avenue was abandoned during a 1938 renovation, in favor of an avenue entrance closer to the elevators.

THIS PAGE, RIGHT:
Alwyn Court lantern on Seventh Avenue: a vestige of the building's original elegance, when it contained apartments of between twenty-two and thirty-five rooms.

RIGHT:
The abundant ornamentation that covers most of the building was facilitated by the use of molds, which could mass-produce terra-cotta decorations. Over the corner entrance and on the decorative panels between the rows of windows can be found the distinctive crowned salamander, a symbol from the festive court of arts patron François I.

AT&T WORLD HEADQUARTERS

Philip Johnson and John Burgee's AT&T World Headquarters, with its towering, arched entrance, its Chippendale bonnet top, and its elegant appointments, has been since its construction one of Manhattan's most controversial skyscrapers. Distinguished for its rich materials, the building, located on Madison Avenue between East 55th and East 56th streets, is clad in slabs of pink granite, with white marble covering the walls of the sky lobby and adjoining executive spaces, and marble and bronze decorating the ample elevator cabs. The lobby contains Evelyn Longman's colossal sculpture, the *Spirit of Communication,* popularly known as *Golden Boy,* which was taken from the top of AT&T's original headquarters at 195 Broadway, dismantled, restored, regilded, and installed in the new, 3-story-high lobby space designed to receive it.

THIS PAGE, TOP:
The 6-story-high loggia entrance of the AT&T Building, by Philip Johnson and John Burgee, 1984.

THIS PAGE, BOTTOM:
The entire building is clad in pink granite.

RIGHT:
Enclosing the gold-leafed statue—taken from the top of AT&T's former headquarters at 195 Broadway—within the new lobby required building the interior space 3 stories high.

CLOCKS

New York City has had public clocks since the eighteenth century, and some of the most impressive ones can be found on Manhattan's public buildings. At the northeast corner of Broadway and Chambers Street, a historic clock marks the old *Sun* Building, which was originally the A. T. Stewart Dry Goods Store, the first of America's great department stores. Over time, the clock's cast-bronze envelope weathered to a lime sherbet green, a patina loved by many, and the timekeeping mechanism stopped. More than a decade ago it was repaired and refurbished by interested volunteers.

The clock atop Grand Central Terminal on 42nd Street is one of the most dependable timepieces in town because it is constantly maintained. It is also one of the largest and certainly one of the most ornate, surrounded by the robust classical figures of Mercury, Hercules, and Minerva, as rendered by French sculptor Jules Alexis Coutan. On the north face of Warren and Wetmore's old New York Central Building, which has stood since 1929 opposite the terminal complex at 46th Street and Park Avenue, two mythological figures by Edward McCartan flank another great clock.

Above the entrance to Tiffany's on the southeast corner of East 57th Street and Fifth Avenue, sculptor Harry Frederick Metzler's standing figure of Atlas has exchanged the world for a globelike clock, which he supports on his shoulders and steadies with his outstretched arms. One block east, at the top of the Fuller Building at 57th Street and Madison Avenue, a clock forms the centerpiece of renowned sculptor Elie Nadelman's *Construction Workers*. Two powerful laborers, naked to the waist and rising above a relief of New York City's skyline, make up the sculptured group over the 3-story entrance, which is supported by a lintel inscribed with the company's name—a fitting motif for one of the largest construction firms in the country at the time.

Colossal lions flank the clock above the entrance to York and Sawyer's Central Savings Bank of 1928 at the northeast corner of West 73rd Street and Broadway. Founded as the German Savings Bank in the City of New York, the name was changed during World War I. But the Teutonic decoration suggested in the winged supports of the clock may contain submerged symbolism related to the bank's original name.

CLOCKWISE FROM TOP LEFT:

The gargantuan illuminated clock atop the Paramount Building on Times Square uses stars in place of numerals (Rapp and Rapp, architects, 1927).

The clock over the entrance to the Paramount Building, 1501 Broadway.

The clock over the 28 Broadway entrance to the former Standard Oil Building of 1922, by Carrère and Hastings; Shreve, Lamb and Blake.

Elie Nadelman's sculpted laborers stand guard beside the Fuller Building's octagonal clock at 41 East 57th Street, Walker and Gillette, architects, 1929.

Central Savings Bank clock at 2100 Broadway, York and Sawyer, architects, 1928.

From the pantheon of mythological figures that grace countless Manhattan entrances; Edward McCartan's reclining gods, by the clock on the New York Central Building.

The old *New York Sun* clock at 280 Broadway, a building that originally housed one of the first major American department stores, the A. T. Stewart Dry Goods Store, and was taken over by the *New York Sun* in 1917. The clock bears the slogan, "The Sun It Shines for All."

OPPOSITE:

Atlas at Tiffany's: here he bears a clock. The 9-foot-tall wooden and lead-footed figure is sheathed in a protective bronze skin. Crafted by Harry Frederick Metzler in 1853 for the first Tiffany's downtown and now on Cross and Cross's 1940 building at 727 Fifth Avenue.

TIFFANY & CO.

THE EMPIRE STATE BUILDING

The Empire State Building was built in 1931 on the site of the first Waldorf-Astoria Hotel. The Waldorf had been built in 1893, and joined by the Astoria in 1897, both designed by Henry J. Hardenbergh. Self-made businessman John Jacob Raskob conceived of the Empire State Building himself, and it was a marketing marvel. Raskob's success in the automotive business had convinced him of the primary necessity of having a superior product and the secondary necessity of being able to make the public believe it was superior.

Designed for maximum efficiency and economy to the plans of architects Shreve, Lamb and Harmon, Raskob indeed had an excellent product. To convince New Yorkers of its superiority he named the building after New York, giving it a strong identity, and gave it an image of integrity by placing the well-connected Governor Al Smith, known for his honesty, at the head of the company. The building flourished, reaching full occupancy almost immediately.

Among the many visual riches of the Empire State Building are the innovative strips of bright metal framing the windows. Replacing the traditional bonding techniques of masonry, the metal strips not only saved precious construction time but also enhanced the building's vertical lines. Since 1977, the building has been celebrating special days, seasons, and events by illuminating its peak with colored lights, using, for instance, green for St. Patrick's Day and red and white for Valentine's Day.

ABOVE, LEFT:
The Empire State Building at 350 Fifth Avenue by Shreve, Lamb and Harmon, 1931—John Jacob Raskob's monument to doing things right with size, style, and efficiency.

ABOVE, RIGHT:
Fifth Avenue façade: the solid geometry of the 102-story building conforms to the traditional organization of a skyscraper into base, shaft, and capital —based on the division of the Classical column. The nearly 6,500 windows are set in framed strips of stainless steel.

OPPOSITE:
The nighttime view, looking south from Fifth Avenue: the tower of the Empire State Building, so named by its developers in the hope of making a lasting impression, is 1,250 feet high.

RESTAURANTS

Manhattan's restaurants represent all types of cuisine, ambiance, and architecture. Delmonico's, founded in 1825 at South William and Beaver streets, became synonymous with aristocratic dining in the nineteenth century. In 1894, Delmonico's opened a restaurant for men only that still stands at the same site. Its main entrance is a kind of reliquary, incorporating ancient architectural elements that were brought from Italy. The architect was James Brown Lord, whose revival of historical styles is most illustriously represented in his Appellate Division Courthouse of 1900 at 25th Street and Madison Avenue.

The Café des Artistes at 1 West 67th Street is one of Manhattan's most popular historic restaurants. At the turn of the century, landscape painter Henry W. Ranger collaborated with builder William J. Taylor to create a cooperative of artists' studios and living quarters on the north side of West 67th Street near Central Park. The Hotel des Artistes near the corner of Central Park West followed in 1917, and its café has been a popular gathering place for artists, musicians, writers, and theater people ever since.

In 1932 one of the country's leading illustrators of the time, Howard Chandler Christy, then living at the Hotel des Artistes, was commissioned to paint a series of murals for the café to brighten its walls. Christy's portrait, by James Montgomery Flagg, another famous artist of the time, hangs near the bar.

Other twentieth-century additions to the restaurant scene in Manhattan include the 21 Club, located in a converted brownstone at 21 West 52nd Street. Of the several clubs that lined the block during the prohibition years, it alone remains. Known then as Jack and Charlie's Place, 21 is easily recognizable by its famous jockey hitching posts outside, recalling the days of horse and carriage.

LEFT:
Airy, springlike Lutèce, at 249 East 50th Street, opened in 1961.

TOP LEFT:
Delmonico's Restaurant, William and Beaver streets, opened in 1825.

TOP RIGHT:
Ichabod's, 2420 Broadway, opened in 1984.

OVERLEAF:
Howard Chandler Christy's lush, fantastic murals for Café des Artistes at 1 West 67th Street were painted in 1932, when the restaurant was already fifteen years old.

FOLLOWING PAGES:
The newly renovated interior of the 21 Club.

Lutèce, specializing in classic French cuisine, was founded in 1961 by Henri Surmain in his home at 249 East 50th Street, a nineteenth-century brownstone. Surmain's chef, André Soltner, bought the restaurant in 1972, when Surmain moved to Spain. A converted pharmacy at 2420 Broadway now houses Ichabod's, which opened in 1984 and serves American grill. J. G. Melon, opened in 1972 at Third Avenue and 74th Street, is a typical New York saloon in the tradition of P. J. Clarke's. Another J. G. Melon opened in 1977 at West 76th Street and Amsterdam Avenue. And Manhattan even has its own 1940s diner—the Empire Diner—opened in 1943, and altered by Carl Laanes in 1976. Its adopted icon, Miss Liberty, announces it at the northeast corner of West 22nd Street and Tenth Avenue in Chelsea.

PRECEDING PAGES:

Nostalgic Café Society, 915 Broadway.

LEFT:

The J. G. Melon Café at 1291 Third Avenue, opened in 1972.

ABOVE:

The Empire Diner, 210 Tenth Avenue, opened in 1943 and renovated in 1976.

THE METROPOLITAN LIFE BUILDING

Though based largely on the design of the famous Campanile in Venice's Piazza San Marco, Napoleon Le Brun's Metropolitan Life tower is elongated and dotted with windows, unlike its Venetian prototype. Erected in 1909, the tower rises above the insurance company's adjacent 11-story headquarters, which Le Brun had built in 1892. The tower replaced the old Madison Square Presbyterian Church, whose congregation had moved across the street to a church completed just three years before by Stanford White. Located at the northeast corner of Madison Avenue and East 24th Street, White's church had been a jewel of resplendent color, with its light terra cotta, yellow brick, gilded details, and granite ashlar of varying hues. Its setting was the pale surfaces of the Appellate Courthouse to the north and the Metropolitan Life tower to the south. But White's church was razed to make way for D. Everett Waid's limestone pile of 1920, which, within a decade, yielded to Metropolitan

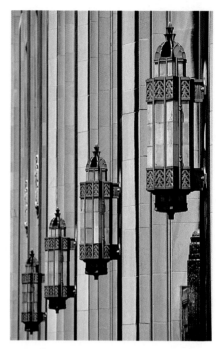

Life's further expansion and the colossal plans of Waid's collaborator, Harvey Wiley Corbett, better known as one of the architects of Rockefeller Center. It stands today in an incomplete state, the base for a much taller building. Corbett set out to create the tallest tower the world had ever seen, but the Great Depression intervened, and what he built in the 1930s, and what we see today is merely the base for Corbett's projected tower of 100 stories.

THIS PAGE, LEFT:
The Metropolitan Life complex at 11–25 Madison Avenue began with Napoleon Le Brun's 1982 headquarters, was topped by Le Brun's 1909 tower, annexed by D. Everett Waid and Harvey Wiley Corbett's building in 1933, and remodeled in 1961–1962 by Lloyd Morgan.

THIS PAGE, RIGHT:
A row of lanterns adorns the 24th Street façade of Waid and Corbett's 1933 building.

OPPOSITE:
The massed forms of the Metropolitan Life Building's southwest corner.

GRAND CENTRAL TERMINAL

To its builders, the ancient figures of Mercury, Hercules, and Minerva atop the façade of the Grand Central Terminal symbolized the city's leadership in contemporary commerce, supported by moral strength and intellectual vigor. Grand Central's main façade, composed of Classical columns and triumphal arches, completes the characteristic Beaux-Arts temple front popular at the turn of the century. The giant limestone structure appears to be floating majestically above 42nd Street, girded by a circumferential plaza, as engineer William Wilgus named the roadway that carries north-south vehicular traffic around it. Entrances on the street lead into the terminal's shops, and gently sloping ramps move pedestrian traffic into the terminal's main waiting room and its Grand Concourse.

Architects Warren and Wetmore created grand interior spaces for the commuters, subway riders, shoppers, and midtown office workers traveling to their various destinations. The variety of services, stores, and restaurants creates a bazaarlike atmosphere, part of the ambiance the designers intended. The architects even included a townhouse for a wealthy friend of the Vanderbilts, which is now the Metro North Police Station House near the Vanderbilt Avenue entrance. And as apartments and clubs grew up around Grand Central, a city within a city was born, called Terminal City—an innovation in urban planning that reached its maturity in the design of Rockefeller Center. The terminal has in recent years become a refuge for New York's many homeless.

RIGHT:
The Roman triumphal arch of Grand Central's main façade easily maintains its dignity when viewed against the towering backdrop of the 59-story Pan Am Building, built in 1963.
OVERLEAF:
Grand Central's main concourse is 470 feet long, 160 feet wide, and 150 feet high, longer than the nave of the Notre Dame Cathedral in Paris.

TRUMP TOWER

Trump Tower's atrium, enclosed by six balconied floors, contains a 5-story, illuminated waterfall. The eye is dazzled by the sheer variety of surfaces, from red marble to burnished bronze, and by the combination of natural light, pouring in from a skylight, and a busy network of designer lighting. The design, by Der Scutt of Swanke, Hayde, Connell and Partners, allows for busy traffic among the host of shops, boutiques, and specialty stores that line the walkways extending from the balconies.

RIGHT:
The 6-level atrium of Trump Tower at 725 Fifth Avenue was completed in 1983 by Der Scutt.

ROCKEFELLER CENTER

Originally planned as a cultural center and a new home for the Metropolitan Opera, Rockefeller Center became an unsurpassed model of urban planning. A cluster of limestone skyscrapers, plazas, shops, garages, and theaters operates as a city within a city—a concept pioneered in Terminal City at Grand Central Terminal. The RCA Building is the centerpiece of the complex, and its sculpture decoration carries the theme of communication. The building faces Fifth Avenue a block to its east and overlooks the sunken plaza that was first made popular as an ice-skating rink, then as an outdoor restaurant during the warmer months. Year round, the plaza acts as an access to the center's subterranean arteries, shops, restaurants, elevators, and stairways, whose stainless-steel fixtures are hallmarks of the Art Deco style of the complex. The sunken plaza is overseen by Paul Manship's gilded figure of Prometheus delivering fire to mankind; his brother Atlas, sculpted by Lee Lawrie, holds

up his armillary sphere in front of the International Building on Fifth Avenue, facing St. Patrick's Cathedral.

One of the most popular attractions of Rockefeller Center is Radio City Music Hall. Decorator and architect Donald Deskey adorned the theater with tall mirrors, two 29-foot-high chandeliers, custom light fixtures, and a golden ceiling. The entrance hall is 140 feet long, 45 feet wide, and 60 feet high, with a grand staircase leading to the balconies above and the lounges below. A stairway mural by Ezra Winter depicts an Oregon Indian legend of man's journey through life, establishing a Native American theme.

Deskey's furnishings for the Radio City lounges are particularly notable. He designed the furniture himself and commissioned painters Yasuo Kuniyoshi for the floral murals in the women's lounge and Stuart Davis for the cubistlike *Men Without Women*, in the men's lounge.

ABOVE:

The RCA Building at 30 Rockefeller Plaza was the first building to go up in Rockefeller Center, which spans Fifth to Sixth avenues from 48th to 51st streets and was built by Reinhard and Hofmeister; Corbett, Harrison and Macmurray; Raymond Hood and Godley Fouilhoux, from 1931–1940. RCA's walls are made of Indiana limestone, and its base is surrounded by a 4-foot-wide strip of Deer Island granite.

RIGHT:

The stairway balustrade gleams from within the black granite lobby of the RCA building.

OVERLEAF:

View from the RCA building of the Rockefeller Center promenade; the complex totals twenty-one buildings.

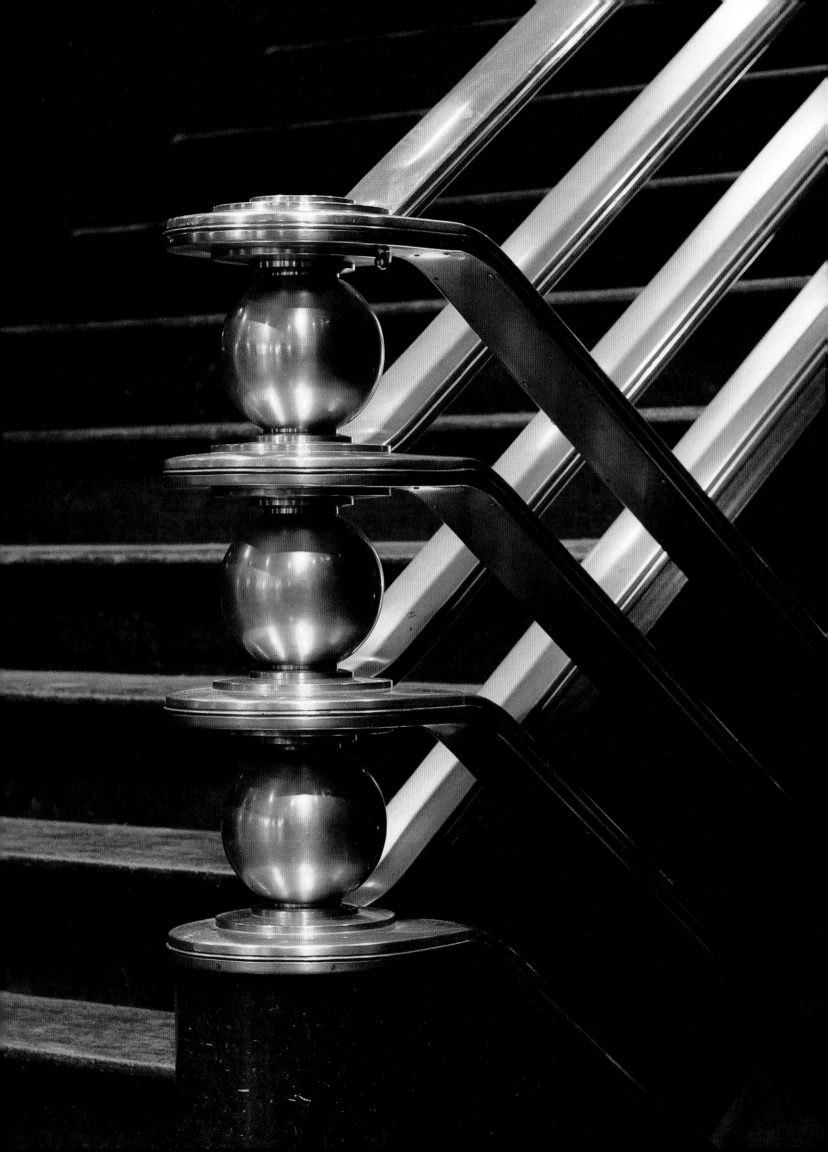

THIS PAGE, TOP:

The Women's Lounge in Radio City Music Hall, designed by Donald Deskey.

THIS PAGE, BOTTOM:

Deskey's Men's Lounge in Radio City contained a mural by Stuart Davis that is now in The Museum of Modern Art.

RIGHT:

A 29-foot-high chandelier over a sweeping staircase and a golden ceiling give Radio City's interior a movie-set glamour.

OVERLEAF, LEFT:

Paul Manship's Prometheus, a bronze-gilded statue 8 feet high and weighing 8 tons, was unveiled in 1934. The ring supporting him bears the signs of the cosmos, the massive base represents Earth. Rising in the background is the RCA building.

OVERLEAF, RIGHT:

Part of the grand sculptural scheme of Rockefeller Center, the 7-ton, 15-foot-high Atlas by Lee Lawrie, 1937, bears the signs of the zodiac on his armillary sphere. In the background are the spires of St. Patrick's Cathedral.

FOLLOWING PAGES:

Sound, one of the low-relief figures on either side of the RCA entrance that symbolizes the essential ingredients of broadcasting.

THE CHRYSLER BUILDING

The Chrysler Building's skin of stainless steel, glass, and brick is punctuated at each setback with symbols old and new. At the base of the tower, a frieze of stylized automobiles, in black-and-white brick, incorporates colossal hub and radiator caps, magnified versions of the 1929 models. Guarding each corner of the building near the top are pairs of repoussé eagles, executed by ironmaster Kenneth Lynch. A giant lotus bud, reflecting the Egyptomania that followed Howard Carter and the earl of Carnavon's 1922 excavation of the tomb of Tutankhamen, emerges near the first setback. The motif is repeated in the lobby, where the elevator doors are decorated with stylized lotus patterns, inlaid with imported woods of eight different tones. Such elegant marquetry extends to the interior of the elevator cabs, there transformed into different designs to provide the building's tenants, as architect William Van Alen explained, with something different on their way to work each day.

The ceiling mural in the Chrysler lobby, by American artist Edward Trumbull, depicts the story of transportation: Figures of laborers and technicians working to produce

THIS PAGE, LEFT:
The mammoth lotus bud near the first setback of the Chrysler Building, 405 Lexington Avenue, William Van Alen, architect, 1930.

THIS PAGE, RIGHT:
From each corner near the top of the Chrysler Building, eagle gargoyles (sculpted by Kenneth Lynch) watch in vigilant pairs.

RIGHT:
East face of the Chrysler Building: stainless steel, glass, and brick, with an illuminated peak. Though part of the original scheme, the lighting was only recently installed.

OVERLEAF, LEFT:
At the pinnacle of the Chrysler tower, a 6-story web of stainless steel arcs over the triangular windows and culminates in a spire that was created within the building and then raised through a special opening. When fully completed in August of 1930 the Chrysler Building measured 1,046 feet high.

OVERLEAF, RIGHT:
Elevator door, the Chrysler lobby: Continuing the Egyptian lotus theme, each of the elevator doors was decorated with woods inlaid in a stylized lotus pattern.

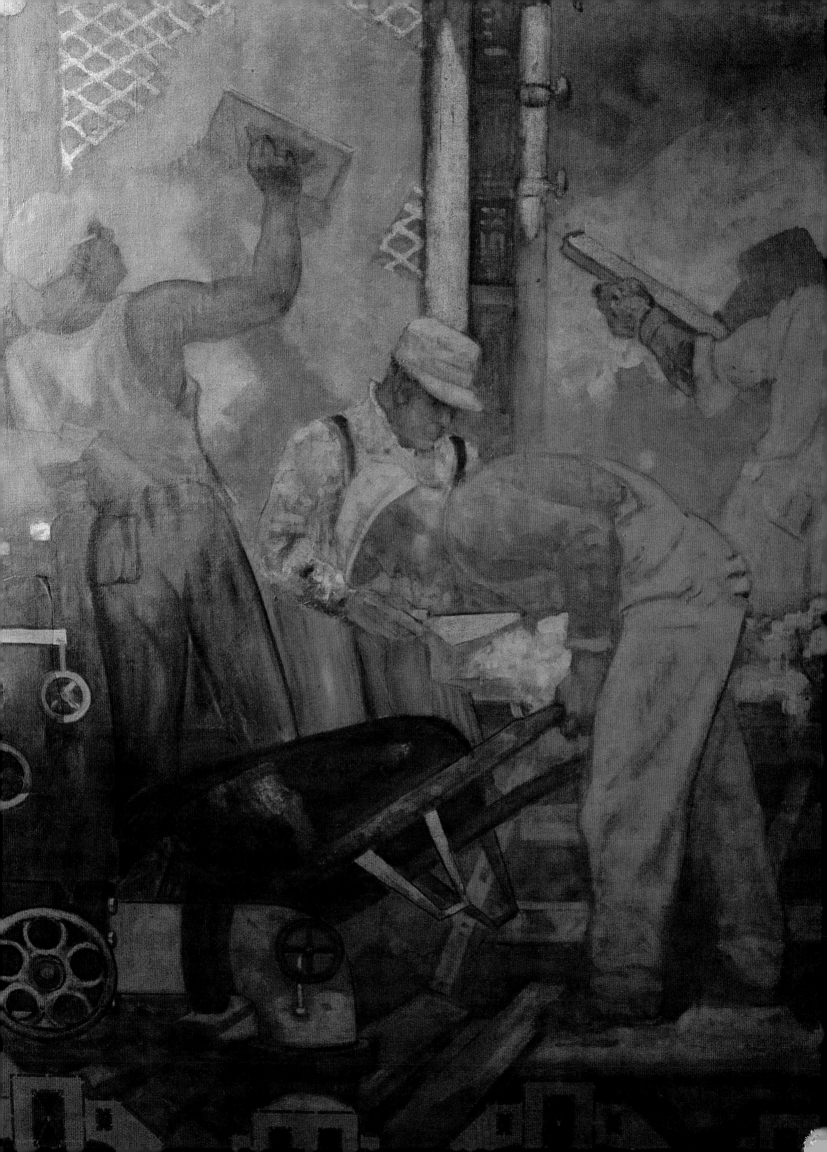

automobiles, airplanes, and locomotives, flank a portrait of the building that extends from the Lexington Avenue entrance to the center of the lobby.

For Walter Percy Chrysler's Cloud Club on the 66th floor, Trumbull painted a trompe l'oeil view of lower Manhattan, giving Chrysler his own piece of the firmament. Against a ceiling of blue sky, stucco was modeled to look like the puffs of great white clouds that passed in front of the windows along the south wall, and above a

sweeping view of the financial district. Trumbull's mural on the side wall widened that view into a panorama, with a breadth that had never before been imagined.

Finally, atop the building, Van Alen's needlelike "vertex" glistens in the morning sun and glows at night, illuminated by the originally planned but only recently installed lighting below, which emanates from the nested chevrons in the building's skin.

PRECEDING PAGES, LEFT AND RIGHT:
The Chrysler lobby ceiling by muralist Edward Trumbull—a stylish tale of transportation in the making.
ABOVE:
The Chrysler Building, from the vantage point of an industrial section of Queens.
RIGHT:
The west face of the Chrysler Building.

CITICORP CENTER

Citicorp Center's 54-story glazed office tower at Lexington Avenue between East 53rd and East 54th streets is boosted into Manhattan's midtown skyline by four giant piers, which shelter a sunken plaza, a subway entrance, and the city's most popular atrium, the Market. Designed by Hugh Stubbins and Associates, Citicorp Center introduced a commercial revival in the midtown east side in the 1970s. The 3-story-high Market, with its gourmet shops, restaurants, home-decorating center, and periodic musical performances, has infused new life into the neighborhood. The tower's angled top, which quickly assumed a unique place in the Manhattan profile, was carefully engineered to be a solar energy collector. Though not enough energy is collected for the massive expenditure of the building's power system, the apparatus is, nevertheless, functional.

ABOVE:
Citicorp Center, at 153 East 53rd Street, built by Hugh Stubbins and Associates in 1977, is a 54-story tower set on four massive piers, with an aluminum trapezoidal roof.

RIGHT:
Citicorp's 3-story skylit atrium, the Market, replete with plants and trees, shops, and restaurants of all kinds.

PAINTED WALLS

Since the 1960s, New York City's walls have provided artists with surfaces on which to exhibit their works, an alternative to the traditional system of galleries and museums.

In the mural at 438 West 37th Street, designed by Tim Hayden and painted by the Evergreene Studio, a glass farmhouse is suspended by a pink ribbon, questioning whether architecture today is on the rise or on the decline. The mural at Forsyth and Delancey streets dramatizes a Puerto Rican community's struggle to succeed in New York, portrayed through a series of vignettes encircled by the flag of Puerto Rico. The mural was developed by the community and executed by artists through the Cityarts Workshop, under the direction of Alan Okada.

A mysterious figure dances atop an image of the Brooklyn Bridge, silhouetted against a building at the corner of Houston and Sullivan streets. A mural at 241 First Avenue at 14th Street advertises bicycles. Even the *Mona Lisa* and the *Statue of Liberty* find themselves lampooned on walls, at 219 West Broadway and the corner of Broome and Thompson streets, respectively.

THIS PAGE:
Top: 241 First Avenue, at 14th Street.
Center, left: The southwest corner of West Houston and Sullivan streets.
Right: Mural on 438 West 37th Street.

RIGHT:
El International Restaurant, 219 West Broadway.
OVERLEAF:
Mural by Stefano at Broome and Thompson streets.
FOLLOWING PAGES, LEFT:
34th Street and Eighth Avenue.
FOLLOWING PAGES, RIGHT:
The story of the Puerto Rican community as told on a wall, 146 Forsyth Street.

PUBLIC BUILDINGS

From the Classical Revival styles of New York City's earliest public buildings to its Postmodern towers of today, the influence of the Ancient, Classical, Renaissance, Medieval, and Baroque worlds on the design of civic buildings is ever present. City Hall, for example, built in 1812 with a colonnaded porch, projecting east and west wings, a broad attic, rusticated basement, and refined architectural detail reflects a sensitive interpretation of Classical forms. This is characteristic of the French Renaissance style that shaped the vision of Joseph François Mangin, the French architect who collaborated with John McComb, Jr. on the building.

Engaged Corinthian columns surround Cass Gilbert's U.S. Custom House of 1907, located at the southern tip of Manhattan across from Bowling Green Park. The decorative fixtures of Charles B. Meyer's Department of Health Building of 1935, at 125 Worth Street, reflect a stylized Art Deco interpretation of the Classical forms that help to identify the building. The ubiquitous American eagle and groups of human figures signify its civic function, which is further emphasized by the inscription of

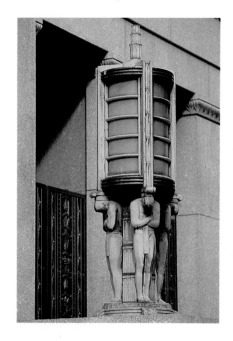 

biblical and modern healers— from Moses to Jenner—which runs along the top of the building on all four sides. And York and Sawyer's Transportation Building of 1926–1927, at Broadway and Barclay Street, echoes the Lombardic influence of medieval Italy. It stands on the site of Isaiah Roger's Astor House of 1834, a Greek Revival masterpiece that was the first modern hotel in New York City.

Among Manhattan's monumental remnants that were once part of a grand urban complex are McKim, Mead and White's General Post Office of 1913 on Eighth Avenue between West 31st and West 33rd streets, and their Pennsylvania Hotel (now the New York Penta Hotel) of

THIS PAGE, LEFT:
The Department of Health Building at 125 Worth Street, Charles B. Meyers, architect, 1935. Lamp standard at the Centre Street entrance, with a section of the grillwork gate in the lower left-hand corner.

THIS PAGE, RIGHT:
Medieval Italian-style civic: ornate lantern at the entrance to the Transportation Building, 225 Broadway, by York and Sawyer, 1926–1927.

RIGHT:
City Hall at City Hall Park, between Broadway and Park Row, Joseph F. Mangin and John McComb, Jr., architects, 1812. In 1831 the cupola was elevated to accommodate a clock and a 6,000-pound bell.

1918, on Seventh Avenue at West 33rd Street. The two buildings were set back from the sidewalk to create a plaza for the firm's since-demolished Pennsylvania Station of 1910, one of Manhattan's most superlative architectural designs, drawn from ancient models that satisfied modern needs.

The two-block-long row of Corinthian columns that forms the main façade of the General Post Office faced a matching row of Doric columns across the street, screening the rear façade of Pennsylvania Station. And the Pennsylvania Hotel's Ionic columns on Seventh Avenue completed McKim, Mead and White's triumvirate of the classical orders.

While many towers of the 1980s do reflect the symmetry of Ancient Classical art, the solemnity of medieval enclosures, the grandness of Renaissance palaces, and the exuberance of Baroque, opulence in the use of costly materials, their exterior surface decoration has been all but eliminated. Their modern façades have been flattened out, like the architect's presentation models that come from the model-maker's studio.

ABOVE:
General Post Office, Eighth Avenue from 31st to 33rd streets, by McKim, Mead and White, 1913, faced by two blocks of Corinthian columns.

RIGHT:
More Corinthian: The U.S. Custom House, at Bowling Green, State, Whitehall, and Bridge streets, by Cass Gilbert, 1907. A steel skeleton and forty-four acanthus-leaved columns.

WOODEN BUILDINGS

After the earliest dugouts with sod roofs and the wickiups of skin and bark, New Yorkers' first houses were of wood or stone. In the Dutch West India Company's seventeenth-century settlement in lower Manhattan, the wood-frame dwellings were built side by side, the first row houses. New York's first farmer-settlers built free-standing houses in stone or wood, or a combination of the two.

Wood-frame and clapboard houses were once plentiful in New York City and continued to be built even after the commissioner's plan of 1811, which imposed a grid system of streets and avenues on New York City's northward expansion. The Dutch also built New York City's first piers of locally hewn timber, which by the early nineteenth century girded lower Manhattan along both the East and Hudson rivers. New Yorkers continued to build and maintain wooden piers into the twentieth century. One of the most interesting is Pier A, at West Street and Battery Place, constructed in 1885, whose clock tower is now a memorial to the dead of World War I.

THIS PAGE, TOP:
Tangible history, the wood-frame houses at 120–122 East 92nd Street are protected by landmark status. Number 120 was built in 1871 and number 122 is a mid-nineteenth-century farmhouse.

BOTTOM LEFT:
The fully operational wooden fireboat house at Pier A, West Street and Battery Place, 1885.

BOTTOM RIGHT:
The bell inside the clock tower of Pier A's fireboat house chimes a steady memorial to the dead of World War I.

OPPOSITE:
The original entrance to 120 East 92nd Street.

TOPS

The 29-story Paramount Building by architects C. W. and George L. Rapp, at Broadway between West 43rd and West 44th streets (1927), supports Manhattan's most famous top. The glass globe, designed as a symbol of the entertainment corporation's worldwide operation, is now used to usher in the New Year. Not only was it illuminated but so too was the clock face below it. Rows of concealed lights at each setback articulated the architect's debt to the great Pre-Columbian pyramids of Meso America, an inspiration for many towers of the 1920s and 1930s.

Raymond Hood's American Radiator Building of 1923, at 40th Street between Fifth and Sixth avenues, is an 8-story tower of black brick atop a 4-story base of polished black granite. The base and tower have gilded details, and the building's golden crown gleams in its nightly light. The black-and-gold color scheme symbolizes the transformation of coal into energy, the mainstay of the American Radiator company. A nocturnal view of the building provided Georgia O'Keeffe with the subject for one of her most evocative works (1927).

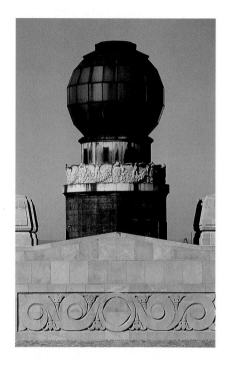

Overlooking the entrance to Central Park at 59th Street and Fifth Avenue, the tops of two Fifth Avenue limestone towers, by architects Schultze and Weaver, bring distinction to the Manhattan skyline and elegance to the Grand Army Plaza. The Sherry-Netherland Hotel of 1926 is capped by an animated François I flèche. To its north is the Hotel Pierre of 1928, with a copper-covered mansard roof that has weathered to a soft lime sherbet green.

The Medieval tower of the Jefferson Market Courthouse of 1877 by Calvert Vaux and Frederick Clarke Withers once served as a fire lookout. The neglected building, restored in

the 1960s, is now a branch of the New York Public Library.

The 40-story-high Fuller Building of 1929 by Walker and Gillette, at the northeast corner of 57th Street and Madison Avenue, was one of the earliest office towers to be placed atop a conglomerate of shops and galleries, an idea that presages Cass Gilbert's U.S. Courthouse of 1936 at Foley Square. Five stories of courtrooms form the base for a 20-story office tower. The Museum of Modern Art's recent design, on 53rd Street between Fifth and Sixth avenues, homogenizes the residential use of the Museum Tower with the exhibition spaces of the museum below.

The juxtaposition of revived Ancient styles is common throughout the city. Gilbert's gilded pyramid atop his Foley Square courthouse and the tholos above McKim, Mead and White's neighboring Municipal Building illustrate the compatibility of Egyptian and ancient Greek forms. A comparison between Gilbert's pyramid and the top of the Park Avenue tower provides useful insight into the survival of Egyptomania, which still pervades Manhattan's tall buildings, and can be traced back to the 1920s. A nondirectional form, the Greek tholos—or circular temple—is particularly suitable as a skyscraper's crowning motif because it is attractive from all angles. When building his 32-story 15 Park Row in 1899, architect R. H. Robertson placed two such forms atop the domes at its north and south ends. The tholos can also conceal water towers—to which the Crown Building of 1921, at the southwest corner of Fifth Avenue and 57th Street, and the San Remo Apartments of 1930, on Central Park West between West 74th and West 75th streets can attest. The Crown Building, with a Gallic cockscomb atop its steep, tiled water-tower enclosure, was originally the Heckscher Building. Designed by Warren and Wetmore, it was the first skyscraper erected after the institution of the 1916 setback law.

Napoleon Le Brun's Metropolitan Life Tower of 1909, based on the Renaissance Campanile from the Piazza San Marco, once struck another dialogue of ancient forms with Stanford White's Madison Square Garden Tower, copied from the medieval Giralda Tower of Seville, and alas no longer standing. Although White's elegant tower and roof-garden domes of Madison Square Garden no longer reign, their influence is echoed in the domes of such neighbors as 1170 Broadway at the southeast corner of West 28th Street.

MUSEUMS

One of the great museums of the world, the Metropolitan Museum of Art at Fifth Avenue and 81st Street can enclose whole buildings. The museum houses the Egyptian temple of Dendur in its Egyptian Wing. Providing a backdrop for the sculpture garden in the American Wing is the complete Greek Revival façade of the Bank of the United States of 1823 by Martin E. Thompson. Saved by the museum when the bank was demolished in 1915, the façade now also serves as the entrance to the American period rooms.

The Cloisters, though part of the Metropolitan Museum, is located in Fort Tryon Park at the northern tip of Manhattan along the Hudson River, facing the New Jersey Palisades. Consisting of a collection of medieval art and architecture assembled by the sculptor George Gray Barnard, the Cloisters was purchased in 1925 with funds donated by John D. Rockefeller, Jr., who also donated land on top of the New Jersey Palisades to the Palisades Interstate Park Commission, to ensure that the view from the Cloisters would always remain intact.

Sculptor and philanthropist Gertrude Vanderbilt Whitney founded the Whitney Museum

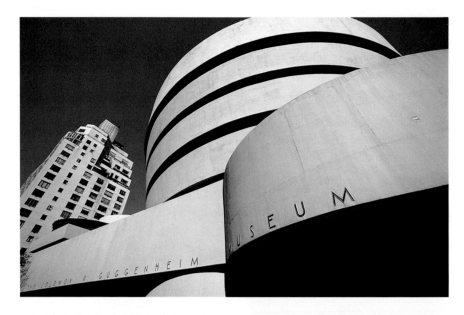

THIS PAGE, TOP:
The creamy concrete Solomon R. Guggenheim Museum, 1071 Fifth Avenue, by Frank Lloyd Wright, 1959.
BOTTOM LEFT:
Marcel Breuer's Whitney Museum of American Art, Madison Avenue at 75th Street, 1966: view from 75th Street, looking south.

BOTTOM RIGHT:
Cesar Pelli and Associates' 1984 glass addition to The Museum of Modern Art at 11 West 53rd Street.
OPPOSITE:
The spiraling interior of the Solomon R. Guggenheim Museum covers more than a quarter of a mile before reaching the 76-foot-round skylight at its pinnacle.

in 1931 at West 8th Street in Greenwich Village. Its present building at the southeast corner of Madison Avenue and 75th Street was designed by Marcel Breuer in 1966. Clad in granite, the museum features a moatlike sculpture garden set below the sidewalk, and the exhibition floors are cantilevered to provide space and light.

The Museum of Modern Art's first home in 1929 was a rented space in the old Heckscher Building (now the Crown Building) at 730 Fifth Avenue.

The Solomon R. Guggenheim Museum is one of Frank Lloyd Wright's innovative elliptical plans. Designed in 1943, it was not built until 1959, after undergoing numerous modifications to satisfy city building codes. The exterior rectangular composition and smooth stucco surfaces relate it to the city's grid and to the surrounding, predominantly limestone apartment buildings. The interior is a series of circular spaces arranged around a continuous ramp. As a permanent exhibition of a Frank Lloyd Wright creation, the work is historically significant and unparalleled. As a museum space, it imposes rigid restrictions on curators.

LEFT, TOP:
The Sackler Wing of the Metropolitan Museum of Art, by Roche, Dinkeloo and Associates, 1978, has a hung ceiling of hammered Misco wire, glass, and aluminum framing.

LEFT, BOTTOM:
The American Wing of the Metropolitan Museum of Art, built in 1980 as part of Roche, Dinkeloo and Associates' expansion plan, houses the Greek Revival façade of the United States Assay office of 1823 by Martin E. Thompson.

ABOVE:
The Cloisters branch of the Metropolitan Museum of Art at Fort Tryon Park, built by Charles Collens from 1934–1938, includes sections of twelfth- and thirteenth-century French and Spanish monasteries.

OVERLEAF:
The Cloisters courtyard.

CHURCHES AND SYNAGOGUES

Congregation B'nai Jeshurun is New York City's oldest Ashkenazic Synagogue (for Jews of German and Polish descent). It was established at 112 Elm Street in 1825, in a break with Shearith Israel, the Sephardic Synagogue (for Jews of Spanish and Portuguese descent). Its temple at 257 West 88th Street, was erected in 1918 to the designs of Walter S. Schneider and Henry Beaumont Herts. In its blend of Egypto-Christian, Moorish, and Roman sources, decorative forms are flattened out almost to the point of abstraction. The revived Semitic character of ornamentation that the architects carried throughout the building marked a turning point in modern synagogue design that continues to influence religious and secular architecture today.

In the Church of the Guardian Angel of 1930, on the northwest corner of Tenth Avenue and 21st Street, architect John Van Pelt captured an authentic flavor of the Italian Romanesque churches of Lombardy in his densely carved friezes, which carry biblical narrative and Christian symbolism.

St. Patrick's Cathedral, by James Renwick, between Fifth and Madison avenues and East 50th and East 51st streets, reads

THIS PAGE, TOP:
Abstracted Egypto-Christian, Moorish, and Roman forms decorate Congregation B'nai Jeshurun (1918), 257 West 88th Street, by Walter S. Schneider and Henry Beaumont Herts.

THIS PAGE, BOTTOM:
Panel of the Church of the Guardian Angel, erected in 1930 at 193 Tenth Avenue by John Van Pelt.

OPPOSITE:
The Church of the Holy Trinity, or Holy Trinity Lutheran Church, Central Park West and West 65th Street, 1903: the Medieval combined with the Classical, and brightened with red doors.

like an encyclopedia of Gothic Revival forms. From its side aisles, canopies of fan vaulting spring from clustered piers, which frame views of the enamellike clerestory windows above the gallery. An elegant flèche marks the Lady Chapel added by Charles T. Mathews in 1906. Lacy spires top the towers flanking the main entrance, and the building's rusticated pier buttresses reassuringly surround the cathedral.

In the Holy Trinity Lutheran Church of 1903, at the northwest corner of Central Park West and 65th Street, ogival arches and flamboyant Gothic detail sensitively relate Medieval carving to the Classical figures in the opalescent, stained-glass windows of the Tiffany and Lamb studios. An equally successful conflation of Classical and Medieval forms is accomplished at the Church of the Transfiguration on 29th Street between Fifth and Madison avenues. Better known as the Little Church Around the Corner, the mid-nineteenth-century structure was built by Frederick Clarke Withers, best remembered for his Jefferson Market Courthouse in Greenwich Village. The architecture is an intimate, English-country Gothic style, and the Edwin Booth Memorial Window by John LaFarge (1898) combines a Medieval subject with Classical forms. Although Booth is anachronistically portrayed as Hamlet, the medieval prince of Denmark, in a Classical setting of Greek and Roman forms, the composition is convincing and the scene is framed with a compatible, Gothic lancet arch.

Riverside Church, on Riverside Drive between West 120th and West 122nd streets and built in 1930 by Allen and Collens and Henry C. Pelton, and the Cathedral Church of St. John the Divine on Amsterdam Avenue at West 112th Street, built by Heins and LaFarge, Cram and Ferguson, are both enormous in scale. They offer limitless opportunity to compare the remarkable varieties in Gothic styles, from Riverside Church's 392-foot-high office tower, topped by its 74-bell Laura Spelman Rockefeller Memorial carillon to its pinnacles, statuary, and decoration, and from St. John's great towers to its cyclopean vaults and boundless sanctuary space, and even to its charming doghouse dormers illuminating the rectory.

A comparison of the carved figures and decorations of the two churches shows how symbolism and narrative can be expressed in different styles. In the scenes carved beneath the statues of the martyrs on the

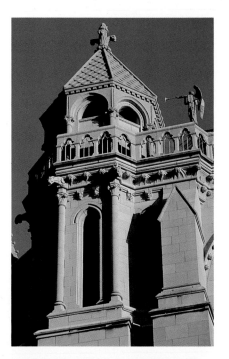

north portal of St. John's, the figures are naturalistically rendered in readable narratives. In one, for example, St. Stephen, the Christian Church's first martyr, twists and turns convincingly as he is being stoned to death. In another, Britain's first martyr, St. Alban, is portrayed in a believable space, protecting a missionary from persecution.

Carved in the tympanum above the entrance to Riverside Church, on the other hand, is the Maesta—Christ in Majesty—a popular symbol of the Middle Ages. The seated figure of Christ is frontal, and his features are stylized like the folds of the garment he wears. Set within a mandorla, a lozengelike halo, his right hand is raised in a teaching gesture and he holds a book in his left hand. More like an icon than a man, the carving style of the figure of Christ at Riverside Church is appropriate for a symbol, which the Maesta is. The figures at St. John the Divine tell stories in sequential series, and the Naturalistic style is appropriate to their purpose.

Riverside Church's repository of stained-glass windows includes a set of original sixteenth-century Flemish windows in the narthex, with scenes from works by Albrecht Dürer, and copies of windows

OPPOSITE PAGE, TOP, LEFT, CENTER AND RIGHT:
A clean Gothic style is maintained in the Riverside Church's statuary and pinnacles.
OPPOSITE PAGE, BOTTOM:
The 74-bell carillon.
THIS PAGE, TOP LEFT:
The Church of the Transfiguration, or Little Church Around the Corner, was built in the mid-nineteenth-century by Frederick Clarke Withers.

THIS PAGE, TOP RIGHT:
A rectory window at St. John the Divine.
BOTTOM LEFT:
The profuse ornamentation on the 392-foot-high Riverside Church tower conceals an internal steel frame.
BOTTOM RIGHT:
Exterior detail, Riverside Church.

in Chartres Cathedral, as well as designs by leading practitioners of the twentieth century, such as Reynolds, Francis, Rohnstock, and Wright Goodhue.

The stained-glass program of St. Patrick's Cathedral is a remarkable compendium of French stained glass by Henry Ely and Nicolas Lorin, in an early-nineteenth-century, Neoclassical style. Crafted as objects of brilliant color to reflect interior light as well as to transmit daylight through them, the glass of St. Patrick's may be seen to advantage at all times of the day and during every season of the year.

Access to light is essential to the life of stained glass and to the interior the glass illuminates. One such oasis, now threatened with extinction by a proposed skyscraper, is the garden of St. Bartholemew's Church of 1919, by Bertram Goodhue, located on Park Avenue between East 50th and East 51st streets. The church's façade, by Stanford White, was brought from its former building at 44th Street and Madison Avenue. In the gable over the main entrance is a medallion with three knives, the symbol of St. Bartholemew's martyrdom.

ABOVE:
The entrance portico of St. Bartholomew's Church comes from the original McKim, Mead and White building of 1902, which was located on Madison Avenue at 44th Street.
RIGHT:
St. Alban protecting a missionary, another carving on the north portal of St. John the Divine.

THE WALDORF-ASTORIA

Schultze and Weaver's Waldorf-Astoria Hotel, located between East 49th and East 50th streets on Park Avenue and capped by its distinctive twin towers illuminated at night, marked the end of an era of elegant hotel building when it was opened in 1931. The only references to the original Waldorf-Astoria—razed in 1929 to make way for the Empire State Building—in this new Art Deco version were the name of the hotel and some of its rooms: Peacock Alley, Empire Room, and Astor Gallery. Enormous in scale for 1931, it rises 47 stories between Park and Lexington avenues, has more than 2,200 rooms, and its services were unparalleled. In addition to restaurants, ballrooms, garden terraces, and hotel and apartment suites, private railroad cars were accommodated on a special siding beneath the hotel. Indirect lighting, coffered ceilings, friezes and carpets by Louis Rigal, monochromatic murals by José Maria Sert, depicting scenes from *Don Quixote*, and the decorations of Arthur S. Vernay and Tony Sarg contributed to its splendor. At the Park Avenue entrance, bas-reliefs by Charles Keck frame the hotel's name, beneath Nina Saemundsson's figure of the *Spirit of Achievement*.

RIGHT:
The Waldorf-Astoria's 625-foot twin towers, built by Schultze and Weaver in 1931, have a private entrance and contain apartments that have housed the likes of dukes (301 Park Avenue, 49th to 51st streets).

GARGOYLES

Ancient peoples placed images of ferocious animals or masks of mythical figures at the entrances to their homes and towns to protect themselves from evil forces. Over the centuries, those images lost their original meanings, but the forms have remained as architectural decoration. The Middle Ages and the Renaissance produced gargoyles, griffins, and hybrids of all description, whose fantastic forms continued to attract architects, sculptors, and designers well into the twentieth century. The François I style, for example, incorporates fauna in its decoration that was particularly popular in many townhouses of the early 1900s. Gargoyles and noble knights decorate the Trinity Building at 111 Broadway, overlooking Trinity Churchyard. Architect Francis H. Kimball employed the Gothic style and decoration on its adjacent twin, the U.S. Realty Building at 115 Broadway, as well, to complement the Gothic Revival Trinity Church nearby. In a medievallike style, historiated (symbolic or narrative) corbels may celebrate or caricature such cerebral subjects as learning and science, or figures may hold objects relating to what the building's owner or tenant manufactures

or sells, as on the Radiator Building.

Classical figures are commonly used for embellishment, and sometimes to carry meaning. Leo Friedlander's limestone relief inspired by Classical and Archaic models, at the entrance to the RCA Building at 49 West 49th Street in Rockefeller Center, tells the story of the communication of the arts through television and radio to the family of man. Caryatids support cornices. A winged Victory displays a banner with the date that Delmonico's opened its restaurant for men only across the street at the site of their original restaurant on South William and Beaver streets. Putti and elaborate garlands decorate townhouse entrances, as on the DeLamar

mansion of 1905 by C. P. H. Gilbert, at Madison Avenue and 37th Street, a building characteristic of the opulence that prevailed in many of the townhouses of the wealthy at the turn of the century. Atop Louis Sullivan's Bayard-Condict Building at 65 Bleecker Street, six angels with arms and wings outstretched occupy the spandrels beneath the roof cornice. They may symbolize the sanctity of the sabbath, watching over workers only six days of the week.

An ensemble of Classical columns and sculpture groups, by Henry Kreis, personifying Music and Art, Comedy and Tragedy, Sport and Industry, and Printing and the Sciences embellish the Hearst Magazine Building on Eighth Avenue, between West 56th and West 57th streets. Designed by Joseph Urban for William Randolph Hearst in 1928, this 6-story building was intended to be the base for another 7 stories. As contemporary accounts have noted, it was conceived as a symbol of Hearst's influence on the reading public, and to be part of the entertainment industry and the arts that were growing up in the neighborhood.

OPPOSITE:
A gargoyle guarding the balcony of Halloran House.

THIS PAGE, TOP LEFT:
Gothic creatures jut out from the top stories of the Trinity Building.

THIS PAGE, TOP RIGHT:
Henry Kreis's sculptural groups at the columns of the Hearst Magazine Building.

BOTTOM LEFT:
A slightly eroded winged victory proclaims the 1894 opening of the men-only Delmonico's, at Beaver and William streets.

BOTTOM RIGHT:
A fantastic sentry sculpted in the François I style guards a townhouse at 3 East 70th Street.

BIBLIOGRAPHY

"Alwyn Court, Harde and Short, Architects." *Architects and Builders Magazine* 10, no. 9 (June 1910): 335.

Barthelmeh, Volker. *Street Murals.* New York: Alfred Knopf, 1982.

Battcock, Gregory and Philip Pocock. *The Obvious Illusion— Murals from the Lower East Side.* New York: George Braziller, 1980.

Bletter, Rosemarie Haag and Cervin Robinson. *Skyscraper Style: Art Deco New York.* New York: Oxford University Press, 1975.

Breck, Joseph. "The Acquisition of George Gray Barnard's Cloisters and Gothic Collections by the Metropolitan Museum of Art." *American Magazine of Art* 16, no. 8 (August 1925): 438–41.

Clark, Kenneth. "The Building of the American Telephone and Telegraph Company." *Architectural Record* 55, no. 1 (January 1924): 81–92.

Corbett, Harvey Wiley. "The American Radiator Building, New York City, Raymond M. Hood, Architect." *Architectural Record* 55, no. 5 (May 1924): 473–77.

"Crystal Palace Graces New York's Skyline." Reprinted from *Building and Construction,* March 1987.

Desmond, Henry W. and Herbert Croly, "The Work of Messrs. McKim, Mead, and White." *Architectural Record* 20, no. 3 (September 1906): 153–246.

Force, Juliana. "The Whitney Museum of American Art." *Creative Art* 9, no. 5 (November 1931): 387–89.

Friedman, Bernard Harper. *Gertrude Vanderbilt Whitney: A Biography.* Garden City, New York: Doubleday, 1978.

Gill, Brendan. Foreword to *The Café des Artistes Cookbook,* by George Lang. New York: Clarkson N. Potter, Inc., 1984.

Gody, Lou, ed. *The WPA Guide to New York City.* Rev. ed. 1939. Reprint, New York: Random House, 1982.

Goldberger, Paul. *The City Observed: New York.* New York: Random House, 1979.

Haas, Richard. *An Architecture of Illusion.* New York: Rizzoli, 1981.

Hall, Edward Hagaman. *A Guide to the Cathedral Church of Saint John the Divine in the City of New York.* 17th ed. New York: The Cathedral Church of Saint John the Divine, 1965.

Hitchcock, Henry-Russell. *Architecture: Nineteenth and Twentieth Centuries.* Baltimore: Penguin Books, 1958.

Hood, Raymond M. "Exterior Architecture of Office Buildings." *Architectural Forum* 41, no. 3 (September 1924): 97–99.

————. "The American Radiator Company Building, New York." *American Architect* 126, no. 2459 (November 19, 1924): 467–84.

"Hotel Pennsylvania, New York." *Architecture and Building* 51 (March 1919): 21–22.

"Hotel Pennsylvania, New York, McKim, Mead, and White, Architects." *Architecture* 39, no. 4 (April 1919): LIII–LVII.

Israelowitz, Oscar. *Synagogues of New York City.* New York: Dover Publications, 1982.

Krinsky, Carol Herselle. "Rockefeller Center." *Antiques* 107, no. 3 (March 1975): 478–486.

————. *Rockefeller Center.* New York: Oxford University Press, 1978.

Landau, Sarah Bradford. "Richard Morris Hunt: Architectural Innovator and Father of a 'Distinctive' American School." In *The Architecture of Richard Morris Hunt,* edited by Susan R. Stein, 47–77. Chicago: University of Chicago Press, 1986.

Lerman, Leo. *The Museum: One Hundred Years and the Metropolitan Museum of Art.* New York: Viking Press, 1969.

Mujica, Francisco. *History of the Skyscraper.* Paris: Archaeology and Architecture Press, 1929.

Oliver, Richard. *Bertram Grosvenor Goodhue.* Cambridge: M.I.T. Press, 1983.

Placzek, Adolf K., ed. *Macmillan Encyclopedia of Architects.* New York: Free Press, 1982.

Reier, Sharon. *The Bridges of New York.* New York: Quadrant Press, 1977.

Reynolds, Donald Martin. *The Architecture of New York City, Histories and Views of Important Structures, Sites, and Symbols.*

New York: Macmillan, 1984.

—————. *Cambridge Introduction to the History of Art: the Nineteenth Century*. London: Cambridge University Press, 1985.

Rorimer, James J. in collaboration with the Medieval Department, Cloisters. *The Cloisters: The Building and the Collection of Medieval Art in Fort Tryon Park*. 3rd ed. rev. New York: Metropolitan Museum of Art, 1963.

Roth, Leland. *A Monograph of the Works of McKim, Mead, and White, 1879–1915*. New York: Arno Press, 1977.

Saarinen, Aline B. *The Proud Possessors: the Lives, Times, and Tastes of Some Adventurous American Art Collectors*. New York: Random House, 1958.

Schultze, Leonard. "The Waldorf-Astoria Hotel." *Architecture* 64, no. 5 (November 1931): 251–308.

Schuyler, Montgomery. "The New Pennsylvania Station in New York." *International Studio* 41, no. 164 (October 1910): LXXXIX–XCV.

Stern, Robert A. M., Gregory Gilmartin, and John Massengale. *New York 1900, Metropolitan Architecture and Urbanism 1890–1915*. New York: Rizzoli, 1983.

Stern, Robert A. M., Gregory Gilmartin, and Thomas Mellins. *New York 1930, Architecture and Urbanism Between the Two World Wars*. New York: Rizzoli, 1987.

Stokes, Isaac Newton Phelps. *The Iconography of Manhattan Island, 1498–1909*. 6 vols. New York: R. H. Dodd, 1915–28.

Tauranac, John. *Essential New York*. New York: Holt, Rinehart and Winston, 1979.

"The Convention Center, a Tour with James I. Freed." *Oculus* 47 (December 1985): 2–17.

"The George A. Fuller Company Building, New York, Walker and Gillette, Architects." *Architectural Forum* 55, no. 2 (August 1931): 185–88.

"The Hotel Pennsylvania, New York." *American Architect* 105 (February 26, 1919): 297–306.

"The International Magazine Building, New York City." *Architecture and Building* 60, no. 10 (October 1928): 303–4.

"The Pennsylvania's New York Station." *Architectural Record* 27, no. 6 (June 1910): 519–521.

The WPA Guide to New York City. Introduction by William H. Whyte. New York: Random House, 1982.

Tompkins, Calvin. *Merchants and Masterpieces: The Story of the Metropolitan Museum of Art*. New York: E. P. Dutton, 1970.

White, Norval and Elliot Willensky. *AIA Guide to New York City*. Rev. ed. New York: Collier Books, 1978.

"World's Greatest Custom House Soon to be Completed." *New York Times* (January 4, 1906): 3.

PAGE 249:
The slender wedge of the Metropolitan Tower at 146 West 57th Street, Harry Macklowe, William Derman and Sheldon Werdiger, designers; Schuman, Lichtenstein, Claman and Efron, architects, 1985.

INDEX

INDEX

Acknowledgments

*All the photographs appearing in
this book were taken with Leica R3
and R4 cameras and Leitz lenses.*

Special thanks to:

*Dora Berenholtz, Michele Carlin,
Duggal Color Projects, Ken Hansen
Photo, Sharon Haspel, E. Leitz
Inc., Harry Macklowe Real Estate,
The Milford Agency, Pamela
Noftsinger, Park Tower Realty,
I. M. Pei and Partners, Louis Shu,
Tishman Realty & Construction,
J. C. Suarès, Vignelli Associates,
and Sheldon Werdiger.*

Prentice Hall Press

*J. C. Suarès
Suzanne Reisel
Laurence Alexander*

*Jane Martin
Leanne Coupe*

Gates Studio